BEASTS & MEN

LECTOR HOUSE PUBLIC DOMAIN WORKS

BEASTS & MEN

JEAN DE BOSSCHÈRE

ISBN: 978-93-90294-92-3

Published: 1918

LECTOR HOUSE LLP
E-MAIL: lectorpublishing@gmail.com

FOLK TALES OF
BEASTS AND MEN

"He Tore A Rib From His Side And Cut Off My Ear"

BEASTS AND MEN
FOLK TALES COLLECTED IN FLANDERS

BY

JEAN DE BOSSCHÈRE

ILLUSTRATED BY
JEAN DE BOSSCHÈRE

1918

CONTENTS

LIST OF ILLUSTRATIONS

Page

There He Met Mistress Goat

UPS AND DOWNS

THE summer had been very hot. Not a drop of rain had fallen for many weeks, and there was drought in the valley where the animals lived. The streams had dried up and the springs had ceased to flow. Master Fox took up his pipe and went out to take a walk under the lime-trees to think things over. There he met Mistress Goat, all dressed up in her Sunday clothes.

"Good morrow, cousin," said he. "You are very fine to-day."

"Yes," she answered, "I put on my best dress because it helps me to think. What we are to do for water I do not know. We have finished all that we had in the barrel, and unless we can find some more very quickly I and my children will die of thirst."

"To tell you the truth," said the Fox, "I was thinking the same thing. I am so dry that my tongue is sticking to the roof of my mouth, and I cannot even smoke my pipe with pleasure. What do you say to going together in search of water? Four eyes are better than two, any day in the week."

"Agreed," said the Goat; and away they started together. For a long time they looked everywhere, but not a trace of water could they find. All of a sudden the Goat gave a cry of joy, and running up to her the Fox saw that she had discovered a well, on the brink of which she was standing gazing at the cool water far below.

"Hurrah!" cried the Fox. "We are saved!"

"Yes," answered the Goat, "but see how far down the water is! How are we to get at it!"

"You just leave that to me," said the Fox. "I know all about wells—I've seen them before. All one has to do is to get into the bucket which is hanging by the rope and descend as smoothly and as safely as you please. I'll go first, just to show you the way."

So the Fox got into the bucket, and the weight of him caused it to descend, while the empty bucket at the other end of the rope rose to the top of the well. A minute afterwards he was at the bottom, leaning over the side of the pail and greedily lapping up the water. Nothing had ever tasted so delicious. He drank and drank until he could hold no more.

"Is it good?" cried Mrs. Goat from above, dancing with impatience.

"It is like the purest nectar!" answered the Fox. "Get into the bucket quickly and come down and join me."

So the goat stepped into the bucket, which immediately began to descend with her weight, while at the same time the bucket with Master Fox in it began to rise to the surface. The two met half-way.

"How is this?" asked Mrs. Goat in surprise. "I thought you were going to wait for me!"

"Ah, my dear friend," answered Reynard with a wicked grin, "it is the way of the world. Some go up and some go down. I hope you will enjoy your drink. Good-bye!"

And as soon as he got to the top he jumped out of the bucket and ran off at top speed.

"I Hope You Will Enjoy Your Drink. Good-Bye!"

So poor Mrs. Goat had to stay there at the bottom of the well until the farmer came and found her, half dead with cold. When at last she was rescued she found that she had only exchanged one prison for another, for the farmer put her into the fold with his own sheep and goats, and so she lost her liberty for ever.

The Farmer Put Her In The Fold

Up And Down

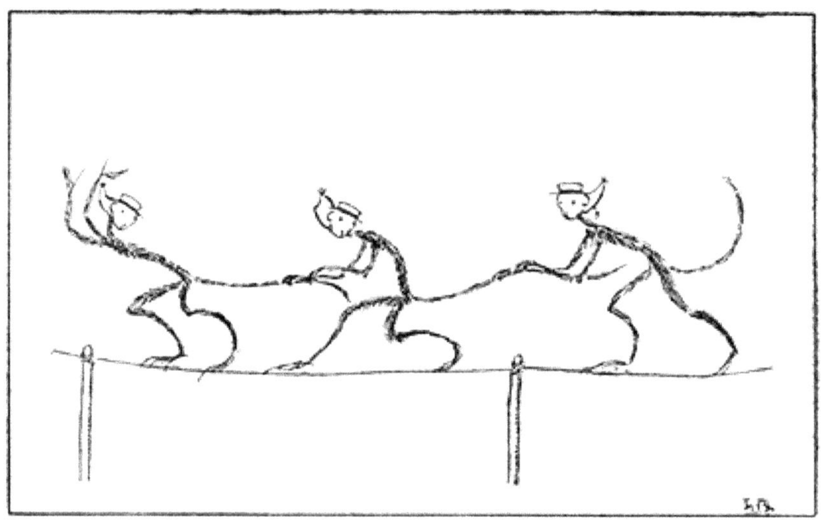

Three Friends

THE THREE MONKEYS

THERE were once three monkeys who were going for a voyage in a balloon. (This was in Monkey-land, far, far away and ever so long ago.) The three were so much alike that it was impossible to tell one from the other, and to make matters worse each of them answered to the name of James. Such a thing would never do in the crew of a balloon, so the old monkey who was in command decided that each of the three should have a different name. The first was to be called James, the second Jemmy, and the third Little James.

So far so good. The three monkeys climbed into the balloon, the ground ropes were untied, and the voyage was begun. When they had reached a height of some hundreds of feet, the captain wished to give an order, so he called to the first monkey: "James!"

"Aye aye, sir," said all the three, running up to him.

"I called James," said the captain, looking from one to the other.

"Well, I am James," answered the first monkey.

"No, no. James is my name," said the second.

"And mine too," said the third.

"How can you be James if I am he?" cried the first angrily.

"I tell you James is my name!" cried the second.

"No, mine!"

And so the three monkeys began to quarrel and dispute. Words led to blows, and soon they were tumbling about all over the car of the balloon, biting, scratching, and pummelling while the captain sat in his chair and bawled to them to stop. Every minute it seemed as though the car would overturn, and the end of it was that Little James got pushed over the side. He turned a beautiful somersault, and fell down, down, down through the air, landing in a soft bed of mud, into which he sank so that only his face and the top of his yellow cranium were visible.

"Help! help!" bawled Little James at the top of his voice.

Up ran a pair of monkeys belonging to the neighbourhood and stood looking at him.

"He's in the mud, brother," said one.

"Up to his neck," said the other. "How silly!" And they both began to grin.

"Help!" cried Little James again, more faintly, for he was sinking deeper, and the mud was nearly at the level of his mouth. "Pull me out! Pull me out!"

"Ah, but how?" asked the first monkey, looking at him gravely.

"Wait a minute," cried the second, "I have an idea!" and he pulled out of his pocket one of those leather suckers on a string which boys use to lift stones. Moistening the disc, he clapped it on to Little James's head, and began to tug on the cord with all his might.

"Hey!" cried the other monkey, running to help. "Pull, brother, pull, and we'll soon have him out!"

Crack! The cord snapped suddenly, and the two monkeys tumbled head over heels. Never mind; they got another cord to repair the damage, and this time they succeeded in pulling Little James clear of the mud.

Did I say Little James? Alas! it was only half of him! His rescuers had pulled so hard that he had broken off short in the middle, and his two legs were left embedded in the mud.

"Dear me!" said the first monkey, scratching his head. "This is very sad. The poor fellow has lost his legs. What shall we do?"

"Let us make him some wooden ones!" said the other.

So said, so done. They made him a beautiful pair of wooden legs, and Little James hobbled painfully home. By the time he reached his house he felt so ill that he went straight to bed. "I believe I am going to die," he said to himself. "I must make my will and set down the cause of my death."

So he sent for pen and paper and began to write. Before very long, however, he stopped and began to scratch his head in perplexity. "If I am going to die," he thought, "I must be going to die of something! Now, what am I going to die of? This must be carefully considered, for above all one must write the truth in one's last testament!"

Little James Got Pushed Over The Side

So he pondered and pondered, but he could not make up his mind as to the cause of his death. Was he going to die of the fall from the balloon, or of his broken legs, or what? Just then he happened to look in the mirror by the bedside, and saw that there was a lump on his forehead, which he had got while fighting with James and Jemmy in the balloon.

"Pull, Brother, Pull, And We'll Soon Have Him Out"

"Why, of course," cried he, "I am going to die of that big bruise on my forehead!" So he wrote it down in his will, and then, happy at having solved the difficulty, turned over on his side and died.

And, as I said before, this all took place in Monkey-land, ever so long ago.

He Happened To Look In The Mirror

Birds

HOW THE GOLDFINCH GOT HIS COLOURS

WHEN the Angel whose mission it was to colour the birds had finished his work, he began to scrape his palette and to make ready for departure. He had done his task well, for the plumage of the feathered creatures all around him glowed with a thousand glorious colours. There was the lordly eagle, arrayed in a robe of golden brown. The peacock had a tail of shimmering blue and green that looked as if it were studded with precious stones. The crow's black coat shone in the sun with a kind of steely radiance, very wonderful to behold. The canary was as yellow as a buttercup; the jay had a spot of blue sky on either wing; even the humble sparrow wore a handsome black neck-tie; while Chanticleer, the cock, was resplendent in yellow, black, and red. All the birds were very proud of their appearance, and they strutted about here and there, gazing at their reflections in the water and calling upon their neighbours to come and admire their beauties.

Alone among the birds the little goldfinch took no part in the rejoicing. Somehow or other the Angel had overlooked him, so that he remained uncoloured, a drab little creature, in his sober grey dress, among the gaily clothed throng. More than once he had tried to draw the Angel's attention to himself, and now, seeing him cleaning his palette in readiness to depart, he stepped forward and said: "Have pity on me, good Angel, and paint my plumage as you have painted that of the others, so that I may walk among them unashamed. I have nothing to commend me — no beautiful song like the nightingale or the throstle, no grace of form such as the swallows have. If I am to go unadorned, nothing remains for me but to hide myself among the leaves."

The Angel Whose Mission It Was To Colour The Birds

Then the Angel took pity on the little creature, and would gladly have painted him with glowing colours, but alas, he had scraped his palette clean. Therefore he took up a brush, and going from bird to bird took from each a spot of colour, which he laid upon the goldfinch, blending a score of brilliant hues with marvellous skill. When he had finished, the tiny bird was transformed, and from being the saddest in that brilliant company he took a place among the most beautiful of them all.

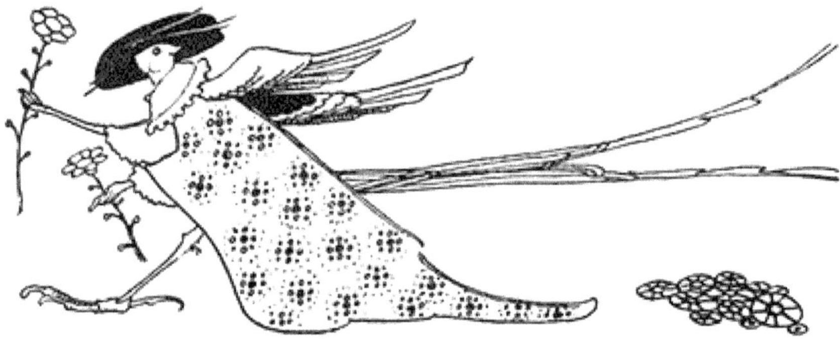

He Took A Place Among The Most Beautiful Of Them All

All The Birds Were Very Proud Of Their Appearance

It is not possible, by means of words, to describe the beauty of the colouring which the Angel gave to the goldfinch, but you may see him any day you like, sitting on a thistle, and chirping his song of gratitude and praise.

Song Of Gratitude

The Fox Was Not A Little Frightened

THE COCK AND THE FOX

THIS is the story that the old woman who was called Tante Sannie told to the little boy who would always be talking:

A long time ago (she said) there lived in a farmyard a Cock who was very proud of himself, and with reason, too, for he was, indeed, a plump and handsome bird. Nothing could have been finer than his appearance when he strutted through the yard, lifting his feet high as he walked, and nodding his head at each step. He had a magnificent comb of coral-red, and blue-black plumage streaked with gold, which shone so brilliantly when the sun flashed on it that it was a joy to see him. No wonder that his twenty wives gazed at him admiringly and followed him wherever he went, and were quite content to let him hustle them about and gobble up all the fattest worms and the finest grains of corn.

If this Cock was proud of his appearance, there was one thing of which he was even prouder, and that was his voice. He was a famous songster; he could crow you high and he could crow you low; he could utter tones as deep as the pealing of the organ in church or as shrill as the blast of a trumpet. Every morning, when the first streak of dawn appeared in the sky, he would get down off his perch, raise himself on his toes, stretch out his neck, close his eyes and crow so loudly that he roused people who were sleeping in the next parish. And this he loved to do, because it was his nature.

Now in the forest close to the farmyard there lived a Fox who had often gazed with longing eyes upon the plump and handsome bird. His mouth watered every time he thought of him, and many were the artful tricks he played to try and catch him for his dinner. One day he hid himself among the bushes in the garden by the farmyard and waited patiently until the Cock happened to stray his way. After a time the bird came along, pecking here and pecking there, wandered through the gate into the garden, and made straight for the bush under which Master Fox was hidden. He was just going to run into the bush after a butterfly which was fluttering about, when he caught sight of Reynard's black snout and cunning, watchful eyes, and with a squeak of alarm he jumped aside, just in time, and hopped on to the wall.

At this the Fox rose to his feet. "Don't go away, my dear friend," said he in honeyed tones. "I would not for the world do you any harm. I know that it is my bad fortune to be disliked by your family—I can't for the life of me think why, and it is a pity, because I have to hide myself for the pleasure of hearing you sing. There is no cock in all these parts has such a magnificent voice as yours, and I simply do not believe the stories they tell about you."

"Eh, what is that?" said the Cock, stopping at a safe distance and looking at the Fox with his head on one side. "What do they say?"

"Why," Reynard went on, edging a little nearer, "they tell me that you can only crow with your eyes open. They say that if you were to shut your eyes, that clarion call of yours would become only a feeble piping, like the clucking of a new-born chick. But of course I don't believe them. Any one can see they are merely jealous."

"I should think so," cried the Cock, bristling with anger. "Crow with my eyes shut, indeed! Why, I never crow in any other way. Just look here—I'll prove it to you!" And he raised himself on his toes, stretched out his neck, closed his eyes, and was just going to crow, when, *Snap!* the Fox sprang upon him and caught him in his teeth!

Then began a great to-do! The poor cock flapped his wings and struggled as the Fox ran off with him. The hens ran about the yard clucking and squawking, and the noise they made alarmed the farmer's wife, who was cooking in the kitchen. Out she came running, with the rolling-pin in her hand, and, seeing the fox with the cock in his mouth, gave chase, shrieking as she ran. The farm-hands tumbled out of barn and byre armed with pitch-forks, spades, and sticks. All the beasts began to raise a clatter, and what with the shouting of the men, the squealing of the pigs, the neighing of the horses, and the lowing of the cows, to say nothing of the clucking of the hens and the old woman's screaming, one would have thought the end of the world was at hand.

The Fox was not a little frightened by all this clatter, but he was not so frightened as the Cock, who saw that only cunning would save his life.

"They will catch us in a minute," he said to the Fox, "and, as likely as not, we shall both be killed by a single blow. Why don't you call out and tell them I came with you of my own accord?"

"A good idea," thought the Fox, and he opened his mouth to call out to his pursuers, thereby loosening his grip on the Cock's neck. Then, with a squirm and a twist and a flutter of his wings, the wily bird wrenched himself free and flew up to the branches of a tree near by.

"Don't Go Away, My Dear Friend," Said The Fox

The Fox cast a look at him and saw that he was out of reach; then he glanced over his shoulder at his pursuers, who were getting perilously near. "It seems to me," he said, grinning with rage, "I should have done better to hold my tongue."

"That is true," said the Cock to himself as he smoothed his ruffled feathers. "And I would have been better advised to keep my weather-eye open."

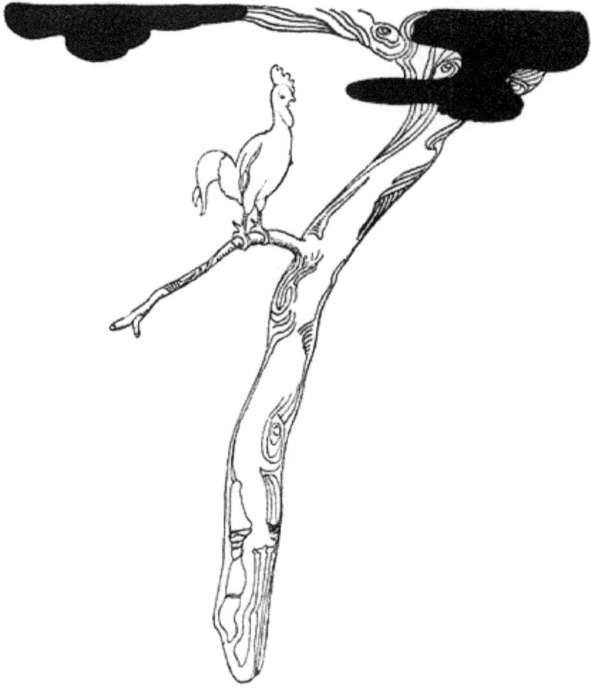

"That Is True," Said The Cock To Himself

The Soldier, The Fox, And The Bear

THE MOST CUNNING ANIMAL

ONE day the Fox and the Bear began to argue as to which was the most cunning animal. The Bear said that he thought foxes and bears took first place.

"You are wrong, my friend," said Reynard. "We are clever, you and I, but there is one animal that is as far above us as we are above the rest of creation."

"Oh, indeed," sneered the Bear, "and what is the name of this marvellous creature?"

"He is called the man-animal," answered Reynard, "and he goes on two legs instead of four, which is a wonderful thing in itself. Here are some of the cunning things he can do; first, he can swim in the water without getting wet; when he is cold he makes yellow flowers grow out of sticks to warm himself; and he can strike at an enemy a hundred yards away!"

"I do not believe you," answered the Bear. "This is a fairy-tale you are telling me. If such a creature as the man-animal really exists, it is very strange that I have never seen him!"

"Strange, indeed!" grinned the Fox, "but soon remedied. Would you like to see the man-animal?"

"It would be a sight for sore eyes," said the Bear.

"Very well," said the Fox, "come along with me." And he led the Bear through the forest until they came to a road leading to a village. "Now, then," said he, "let us lie down in the ditch and watch the road, and we shall see what we shall see."

Presently a child from the village came along.

"Look! Look!" whispered the Bear. "An animal walking on two legs! Is this the creature we seek?"

"No," answered the Fox, "but one of these days it will become a man-animal."

Shortly afterwards there came along an old woman, all bent and wrinkled.

"Is that one?" asked the Bear.

"No," said the Fox again, "but once upon a time that was the mother of one!"

At last there came the sound of brisk footsteps on the road, and peeping out between the bushes the Bear saw a tall soldier in a red coat marching towards them. He had a sword by his side and a musket over his shoulder.

"This must surely be the man-animal," said the Bear. "Ugh! what an ugly creature! I don't believe he is cunning in the least!" But the Fox made no answer, for at the first sight of the soldier he had fled into the forest.

"Well, well," muttered the Bear, "I don't see anything to be afraid of here. Let us have a talk with this wonder!" And hoisting himself clumsily out of the ditch he lumbered along the road to meet the soldier.

"Now then, my fine fellow," he growled, "I have heard some wonderful stories about you. Tell me...."

But before he could get another word out of his mouth the soldier drew his sword and struck him such a shrewd blow that he cut off his ear.

"Wow!" cried the Bear, "what's that for? Tell me...." But then, seeing the gleaming steel flash once again, he turned tail and ran off as fast as he could go. Just as he reached the edge of the wood, he looked backward and saw the soldier raise his gun to his shoulder. There was a flash, a loud report, and the Bear felt a terrific blow against his side. Down he went like a ninepin, but fortunately for him the bullet had merely glanced off his hide, and he was not seriously hurt. Picking himself up, he lost no time in gaining the shelter of the trees, and presently came limping painfully to the place where the Fox was waiting for him.

"Well, my friend," said Reynard, "did you see the man-animal? And what did you think of him?"

"You were right," answered poor Bruin sadly. "He is certainly the most cunning creature in the world. I went up to speak to him and he tore a rib from his side and cut off my ear. Then I ran away, but before I could reach the trees he picked up a stick and pointed it at me. Then there came thunder and lightning, and a piece of the earth heaved itself up and knocked me spinning! Beyond all doubt the man-animal takes the palm for cunning, but I never want to see him again, for I shall carry the marks of our first meeting to my dying day."

And Reynard grinned, and said: "I told you so!"

There Was A Flash, A Loud Report.

The Two Heroes Of The Story

SPONSKEN AND THE GIANT

THERE was once a lad whose face was so badly pitted by the smallpox that everybody called him Sponsken, which means little sponge. From the very day of his birth Sponsken had been a great cause of anxiety to his parents, and as he grew older he became more trouble still, for he was so full of whims and mischief that one never knew where one had him. He would not learn his lessons, nor work at any serious task for ten minutes on end. All he seemed to think of was cutting capers and playing practical jokes on people. At last, in despair, his parents told their trouble to the village sexton, who was a great friend of the family, and often came to smoke his pipe with Sponsken's father in the chimney corner.

"Don't worry, my friends," said the sexton. "I've seen young men like your son before, and they are quite easy to manage if one only goes about it the right way. Just leave him to me. What he wants is a good fright, and I'll make it my business to see that he gets it."

So far so good. Sponsken's parents were only too glad to fall in with any plan which seemed likely to reform their unruly son, so the sexton went off to make his arrangements. That night he whitened his face with flour, covered himself in a white sheet, and hid behind a tree on a road along which he knew Sponsken would have to pass.

It was the dark of the moon, and the place the sexton had chosen was very lonely. For a long time he waited; then, hearing Sponsken coming along whistling a merry tune, he sprang out suddenly from behind his tree and waved his arms in a terrifying manner.

"Hallo!" said Sponsken. "Who are you?"

The sexton uttered a hollow groan.

"What's the matter?" said the boy. "Are you ill? If you can't speak, get out of my way, for I am in a hurry."

The sexton groaned again, louder than before, and waved his arms wildly.

"Come, come," cried Sponsken, "I can't stay here all night. Tell me what you want at once and let me pass." Then, as the ghostly figure made no answer, he struck it a blow with the stout ash-stick which he carried, and the poor sexton fell, stunned, to the ground. Sponsken stayed long enough to take a glimpse of the ghost's face and to recognize the features of the sexton beneath the flour; then he went on his way homeward, whistling as merrily as before.

When he reached home his parents gazed at him uneasily. They were very anxious about the success of their friend's plan, but Sponsken did not look at all like a lad who had been frightened—quite the contrary in fact, for he drew his chair up to the table and set to work upon his supper with an excellent appetite.

"A funny thing happened to me to-night," he said carelessly between two bites of an onion. "As I was walking along the lonely road by the cemetery a white figure jumped out at me."

"A wh-white figure!" stammered his father. "How terrifying! And what did you do, my son?"

"Do?" said Sponsken cheerfully. "Why, I fetched him a crack on the skull with my staff. He went down like a ninepin, and I warrant he won't try to frighten travellers again!"

"Base, ungrateful boy!" cried his father, rising to his feet. "It was my dear friend Jan the sexton you struck. All I hope is that you have not killed him."

"Well, if I have, it is his own fault," answered Sponsken. "He should not play tricks on me." But his father continued to rage and grumble so long that Sponsken got tired of hearing him at last, and flung off to bed in a sulk.

"I'll stand no more of this," he said to himself. "Since my own people do not appreciate me, I'll go out and seek my own fortune in the world, and they may go on as best they can."

The next morning, therefore, having packed a loaf of bread and a piece of cheese in a bag, Sponsken set off on his travels, telling nobody where he was going, and taking nothing else with him except a sparrow which he had tamed and kept since it was a fledgling. After walking for a long time he came to a forest, and feeling rather tired he sat down on the trunk of a fallen tree to rest.

Now in this forest lived a giant who was the most hideous creature one could possibly imagine. From his forehead jutted a pair of horns; his features were more like those of a beast than a man, and his finger-nails grew long and curved like the claws of a wild animal. The giant considered himself lord of the whole wood, and was very jealous lest anybody should enter his domain. When, therefore, he saw

Sponsken he was very angry, and having pulled up a young tree by the roots to serve him as a club, he approached the young man, who was sitting with his eyes closed, and struck him a heavy blow on the shoulder.

Sponsken, The Giant, And The Princess

In spite of appearances, Sponsken was not asleep; he was far too wary a person to be caught napping under such conditions. As a matter of fact, he had seen the giant before the giant saw him, and he knew that his only chance of escape was to remain unperturbed and calm. When, therefore, the giant struck him on the shoulder, he opened his eyes sleepily, rubbed the place, and said with a yawn: "A pest on these flies! They bite so hard that a fellow can't sleep for them."

"You shall sleep soundly enough in a minute!" muttered the giant, who was enraged at Sponsken's nonchalance. "See how you like this!" And he gave the lad a blow on the other shoulder, harder than before.

"There they are again!" cried Sponsken, rubbing the place. "My word! They bite even harder on this side than on the other. It is time I was going!" And he rose from his seat, starting back with surprise as he affected to see the giant for the first time.

"So it's you, is it?" he cried. "What do you mean by tickling me when I am trying to sleep? If I were not so kind-hearted I'd break your neck for you!"

"Have a care what you say," cried the giant. "Do you know that I have the strength of twenty men and could crush you between my hands like a kitten?"

"Pooh!" said Sponsken. "Words are windy things. I have no doubt you could kill a whole regiment with your breath. But words won't go with me, my man; you must give me some proof of your prowess."

"Proof!" roared the giant. "See here! I can throw a stone so high into the air that it will not come down for a quarter of an hour." And he was as good as his word, for, picking up a large stone, he flung it with all his strength, and it was more than a quarter of an hour before it fell again at their feet.

"Can you match that?" asked the giant with a grin.

"Easily," said Sponsken. "I will throw a stone so high that it will not come down at all!" Bending to the ground he picked up a pebble and showed it to the giant, but very cleverly he managed at the last moment to exchange it for the sparrow which he carried in his pocket, and this he was able to do because the giant was rather short-sighted, and, if truth be told, slow-witted as well.

"One, two, three!" cried Sponsken, and he tossed the bird into the air, and of course it flew up and up and never came down at all.

"Well, well," said the giant, "I never saw such a thing as that in my life before. You are certainly a wonderful stone-thrower, little man. But can you do this?" And picking up another stone, he squeezed it so hard between his immense fists that he crushed it into a fine powder.

"Yes, that is hard to do," said Sponsken, "but I think I can go one better. Any oaf, if he be strong enough, can crush a stone to powder, but it requires skill as well as strength to wring the juice out of one. Watch me!" So saying, Sponsken adroitly slipped out his piece of cheese, and squeezed it until the whey dripped from between his fingers.

He Tossed The Bird Into The Air

"The Three Animals Are A Bear, A Unicorn, And A Wild Boar"

"Marvellous!" said the giant. "I confess myself beaten. Let us go into partnership, for there cannot be two others like us in the whole world."

"Willingly," answered Sponsken, "but what are we to do?"

"Why, as for that," said the giant, "the King of this country has promised his daughter's hand in marriage, and a great treasure besides, to anybody who can destroy three ferocious beasts which are devastating his realm. It seems to me that this is a task we can quite well do together. You, with your quickness and skill, can trap the beasts, and I can kill them with my club. That done, we will divide the spoils."

So it was agreed, and without wasting a moment the two took the wood together. Before very long they reached the King's palace, and sent up a message by one of the lords in waiting that they would like to see His Majesty.

"And do you mean to tell me," asked the King, when he had heard the giant's tale, "that you can overcome the three fierce animals by the help of this ugly little pock-marked fellow."

"Hush! Not so loud, for the love of heaven!" whispered the giant. "My friend is very touchy about his appearance, and if he hears you making such slighting remarks it is very likely he will bring the whole of your palace down about your head!"

The Bear Followed Him Into The Hollow Trunk

"You don't say so!" whispered the King in reply, glancing fearfully at the terrible little man. "Well, you are at liberty to try your luck. The three animals are a bear, a unicorn, and a wild boar, and at present they are hidden in the wood close by. There you will find them, but take care of yourselves, for they have already killed scores of my men."

"Don't be afraid," answered the giant, "for us this is as easy as playing a game."

After having partaken of a good meal the two made their way towards the wood in which the animals were hidden.

"We must make a plan," said Sponsken. "Listen to what I propose. You go into the middle of the wood while I remain here on the outskirts; then when you drive the beasts out I will see that they do not escape."

So it was arranged. The giant went forward into the wood, while Sponsken remained outside, waiting to see what would happen. He had not to wait long, for presently there was a crashing and a tearing of undergrowth and a great bear came lumbering towards him. Sponsken did not like the look of the creature at all, and decided to put as much space between them as possible. Looking here and there for a refuge, he spied a big oak-tree, and quickly climbed its trunk and ensconced himself among the branches. Unfortunately the bear had already seen him, and, raising himself on his hind legs with a dreadful roar, he rushed to the tree and began to climb. In another moment Sponsken would have been lost, but by good chance the tree happened to be hollow, so without hesitation the lad let himself down into the trunk, and finding at the bottom a small hole which led to the open air, he was just able to wriggle through it and escape. The bear followed him into the hollow trunk, but the hole at the bottom was too small for him to get out by, and as there was hardly room to move inside the trunk, the angry creature had to stay where he was, waking all the echoes in the forest with his growling.

The next minute the giant came running out of the forest. "Have you seen the bear?" he cried. "I drove him towards you!"

"Don't worry," answered Sponsken coolly; "I've shut him up in the tree there to keep him safe."

The giant rushed to the tree and dispatched the bear with one blow of his great club. Then, pulling out the carcass, he shouldered it, and the two went back to the palace, congratulating each other on the excellent beginning of their enterprise.

There remained now the unicorn and the wild boar. Next day Sponsken and the giant went to the forest again, and since their first plan had been so successful, it was arranged that they should follow exactly the same course. The giant went into the depths of the wood to find the unicorn and drive him out, while Sponsken remained on the borders to capture the animal when he came.

This time the period of waiting was longer, and Sponsken, leaning against the oak-tree, had almost fallen asleep when a clattering of hoofs awakened him, and he sprang aside just in time to escape the unicorn, who, breathing fire from his nostrils, charged down upon him. So great was the impetus of the beast's charge that he could not stop himself, and with a mighty crash he ran full tilt into the tree, driving his horn so far into the trunk that, although he pulled and struggled, he could not wrench himself free.

With A Mighty Crash He Ran Full Tilt Into The Tree

When the giant came up, Sponsken showed him the animal, which was quickly killed with a single blow of the club.

"Didn't I manage that affair well?" asked Sponsken as they went back to the palace.

"You are a wonder!" answered the giant, and he really believed what he said.

Now only the wild boar remained, and on the following day the two went to the forest to capture him also. Once again the same plan was followed, but this time Sponsken kept his eyes wide open, and when the ferocious beast broke cover he ran as fast as he could in the direction of the royal chapel. The wild boar followed him, and a fearsome creature he looked, I assure you, with his wicked little eyes and his great curved tusks and the hair on his back bristling like the quills of a porcupine.

Through the open door of the chapel Sponsken ran, and the boar, snorting with fury, followed him. Then began a fine chase, round and round the aisles, over the pews, and in and out of the vestries. At last Sponsken seized a chair, and dashing it against a window broke several panes, and so made good his escape. While the boar was still standing stupidly staring at the hole through which he had gone out, Sponsken ran round to the door, which he closed and locked. Then, having broken one or two more panes of glass, he sat down quietly by the chapel wall and began to pare his nails.

A short time afterwards the giant came rushing up.

"Where is the boar? Have you let him get away?" he cried.

"Don't get so excited," answered Sponsken. "The boar is safe enough. He's in the chapel there. I had no other place to put him, so I flung him through the window!"

"What a wonderful little man you are!" said the giant gleefully, and he ran off to kill the boar with one blow of his club. This done, he hoisted the carcass on to his shoulders and took the road to the palace. Half-way there the weight of the boar began to tell, for it was a massive beast, and the giant was forced to stay and rest.

"It is all very well," said he, mopping his streaming brow, "but I think you ought to take a turn with me in carrying this carcass."

"Not I," answered Sponsken. "We made an agreement that my work was done when I captured the beast, and I intend to keep to it."

Sponsken The Princess The Giant

So the giant had to struggle on as best he could for the rest of the way, grumbling at every step, while Sponsken followed, laughing up his sleeve, and exceedingly thankful that he had escaped the task.

When they reached the palace the two presented themselves before the King and claimed the promised reward. But now a difficulty arose. It was quite easy to divide the treasure, but which of them was to have the Princess?

"I think it should be I," said the giant, "for I killed the three animals."

"Not at all," said Sponsken. "The Princess should be given to me, for I captured the beasts."

"A lot of good your capturing them would have been if I had not killed them!" said the giant.

"How could you have killed them if I had not caught them first?" answered Sponsken. And so the two began to quarrel, and neither would give way, and high words passed between them. Truth to tell, the King was not at all sorry that the dispute had arisen, for he did not very much relish the idea of his daughter marrying either the bestial giant or the pock-marked, ugly little fellow who was his companion.

"There is only one way out of the difficulty," said the King at last. "We must let fate decide. Listen to the plan I propose. You shall both of you sleep in the Princess's chamber to-night—the giant in a bed on one side of her couch, and Sponsken on the other. I also will remain in her chamber and watch her carefully. If she spends most of the night with her face turned towards Sponsken, it shall be a sign that she is to marry him; if, on the other hand, she favours the giant, he shall be her husband; but if she sleeps all night with her face towards neither of you, then you must both give her up, and be satisfied with the treasure."

So it was agreed, and that night the trial took place. Sponsken, however, did not by any means intend that blind chance should settle so important a matter, and he spent the intervening time in making certain preparations. First of all he went to the palace gardens, from which he gathered certain herbs having an aromatic and beautiful perfume; these he placed in a bag and hid under his clothes. Then from the woods he gathered all the herbs he could find which had a disagreeable smell, such as garlic and stinkwort and poisonous fungus; these also he placed in a bag, and seized an early opportunity, when they came to the Princess's chamber, of hiding the bag under the pillow on which the giant's head was to rest.

The Princess well knew the fateful issue which was to be decided in the night, and as she had firmly made up her mind not to marry either the one or the other of her suitors, she determined to remain awake all night and to take care to keep her face turned towards the ceiling. For a time she managed to do so, but before long drowsiness overcame her, and she slept. Presently she turned over on her left side and lay with her face turned towards the giant, who began to chuckle to himself.

"Wait a minute," thought Sponsken. "I don't think the Princess will keep that position long!" And sure enough, the horrible stench of the herbs in the bag beneath the giant's pillow penetrated even to her dreams, and the Princess turned over hurriedly on the other side. What a change was there! Instead of a disgusting smell which made her dream of gloomy caverns and noisome things, she found now a delicious perfume that brought pictures of sunlit gardens all glowing with flowers and bright-winged butterflies flitting over them. The Princess gave a little sigh of content, and for the rest of the night she remained with her face turned towards Sponsken, so that the King had no choice but to declare the little man the winner.

The Princess, however, refused to abide by the judgment. "I will *not* marry that vulgar fellow," she cried. "I will die first! Oh, father, if you love me, think of a means of escape!"

"Do not be afraid, my child," answered the King. "I will arrange something." And the next day he took the giant aside and proposed to him that he should rid him of Sponsken, promising a rich reward for the service. The giant's greed was aroused, and being very jealous of his companion's success, he was the more ready to fall in with the King's suggestion.

Fortunately for himself, Sponsken's quick wits made him suspicious. He guessed that some treachery was afoot, and in order to be prepared for emergencies he took a heavy hammer with him when he retired to bed at night. His suspicions were justified, for towards midnight the door of his room opened and the giant entered on tiptoe, carrying a heavy axe with which he intended to dispatch our friend. No sooner was his foot inside the door, however, than Sponsken jumped out of bed and sprang at him, looking so fierce that the giant, who was a coward at heart, and had besides a healthy respect for his companion's powers, turned and fled in dismay. Then Sponsken lifted his heavy hammer and struck three resounding blows upon the floor. The noise awoke everybody in the palace, and servants, guards, and lords in waiting came flocking to the room to discover the cause. The King came last of all, a little anxious about the success of his fine plot, and when he found Sponsken sitting up in bed, quite unharmed, his face fell.

"What is the matter?" he stammered.

"Matter?" answered Sponsken. "Nothing very much! Some person wandered into my room, so I just gave three taps with my fingers on the wall. It is lucky for you all that I did not strike the blows with my fist, for had I done so I am afraid there would have been nothing left of your palace but a heap of dust!"

At these words everybody turned pale, and the King made haste to protest his undying friendship for his terrible guest.

As for the giant, he was in such fear of encountering Sponsken's resentment that he fled, and nobody ever saw him again.

Now the poor King did not know what to do, for his daughter still persisted in her refusal to marry Sponsken, and he was torn two ways by love and fear. Just at that time, however, a neighbouring monarch, who was an old enemy of the King's, declared war upon him, and this offered another opportunity for delay. Calling Sponsken before him, the King proposed that he should prove his valour by challenging the enemy king to mortal combat. Sponsken agreed; but his fame had already been noised abroad, and the challenge was refused.

"Very well," said the King, who was at the end of his resources. "As my prospective son-in-law you ought to lead my armies into battle. I will place my own charger at your disposal, and I look to you to save my country from defeat."

Here was a pretty kettle of fish! Sponsken had never ridden a horse in his life, and he had not the slightest knowledge of warfare. To make matters worse, the steed in question was a notoriously vicious brute who would allow nobody but his own master to mount him. Already he had accounted for several grooms and stablemen, whom he had kicked to death.

Sponsken commanded that the steed should be led to the borders of the forest and tied by the bridle to a tree. He had not the slightest intention of trying to mount the brute, and his plan was to wait until the attendants had gone away and then to slip off unobserved. Fate, however, was too much for him, for hardly was the horse safely tied up than couriers came spurring along the road to say that the enemy king was advancing at the head of his army, and was at that very moment less than half a mile away.

All The Attendants Fled At Once

All the attendants fled at once, and Sponsken himself was so overcome by terror that, without thinking what he was doing, he jumped upon the back of the steed, and, forgetting that it was tied to the tree, dug his sharp spurs into its side. The horse plunged and reared, champing at the bit and doing its best to dislodge Sponsken from the saddle, but the lad clung on for dear life. At last, finding all its efforts unavailing, the horse dragged the tree up by the roots and charged forward in a straight line towards the advancing enemy. Almost dislodged from his seat by the sudden jerk, Sponsken stretched out his hand and grasped the branches of the tree, which swung in a terrifying manner at his side, promising every moment to hurl him from the saddle, and the result was that to the enemy army it appeared as though he were charging down upon them at full speed, bearing a tree as a club. Filled with dismay at the terrifying sight, the soldiers of the enemy king fled in all directions and hid themselves in the woods and in the crevices of the rocks. Sponsken rode on for the simple reason that he could do nothing else, right into the enemy's camp, where the steed came to a standstill and our hero was able to jump down from its back. Entering the king's tent, he helped himself to all the documents and articles of value he could find; then, having cut the tree from the bridle, he remounted the horse, which was now quite tame and docile, and rode back to the palace.

When the King heard that the enemy was routed he was overjoyed, and he recognized that a man who could perform such a feat single-handed was not to be treated lightly. His daughter, however, was still firm in her refusal to marry Sponsken, and so the King made him an offer of half his kingdom if he would release him from his promise and allow the Princess to go free. Sponsken accepted his terms and married a girl who, although she was not a princess, was nevertheless very pretty. Their wedding was celebrated with great pomp and they lived together very happily for the rest of their lives.

Married A Girl

The Cat And The Sparrow

WHY CATS ALWAYS WASH AFTER EATING

A LONG time ago a cat caught a sparrow, and licked his lips in anticipation of the delight he would feel in devouring it. After playing with it for a time, as cats will, he was going to eat it, when the sparrow spoke to him.

"The Emperor's cat," said the sparrow, "and all his family, never begin a meal without washing themselves first. Everybody knows that such is the custom in polite society."

"Really," answered the cat, "well, I will do as the Emperor's cat does!" And he let go the sparrow and began to wash his face. Feeling itself free, the sparrow flew away, and alighted safely on the branch of a tree well out of reach.

"It serves me right," muttered the cat, "for being so easily taken in."

And ever since that time cats have always washed themselves after their meals.

"I've Just Been Turned Out Of House"

THE CHORISTERS OF ST. GUDULE

THE miller of Sandhills had a donkey which had served him well in its time, but was now too old to work. The miller was a careful man, who did not believe in feeding useless mouths, so he decided that he would sell the donkey for the price of its skin. "I do not suppose I shall get very much for the wretched beast," he said, regarding poor Greyskin as he stood with hanging head in his stall, "but I shall save the cost of his corn anyhow, and that is always something."

Left alone, Greyskin reflected sadly upon the fate in store for him. "Such is the way of the world," he thought. "When I was young and hearty nothing was too good for me; now I'm old and useless I am to be cast out. But am I so useless after all? True, I can no longer pull a cart to market, but I have a magnificent voice still. There must be a place somewhere for one who can sing as beautifully as I. I'll go to the Cathedral of St. Gudule, in Brussels, and offer myself as a chorister."

Greyskin lost no time in acting upon his resolve, but left his stable immediately and set out on the road to Brussels. Passing the Burgomaster's house he saw an old hound sitting disconsolately on the doorstep.

"Hallo, friend!" said he. "What is the matter with you? You seem very sad this morning."

"The matter is that I am tired of life," answered the dog. "I'm getting old and stiff and I can no longer hunt hares for my master as I used to do. The result is that

I am reckoned good for nothing and they grudge me every morsel of food I put into my mouth."

"Come, come, cheer up, my friend," said Greyskin. "Never say die! I am in a similar case to yourself and have just left my master for precisely the same reason. My plan is to go to the Cathedral of St. Gudule and offer my services to the master of the choir. If I may say so without conceit, I have a lovely voice—one must make the most of one's gifts, you know—and I ought to be able to command good pay."

"Well, if it comes to that," said the dog, "I can sing too. I sang a lovely song to the moon last night, and if you'll believe me, all the people in our street opened their windows to listen. I sang for quite an hour, and I'd have gone on longer if some malicious person, who was no doubt jealous, had not thrown an old boot at my head."

"Excellent," said Greyskin. "Come along with me. You shall sing tenor and I'll sing bass. We'll make a famous pair."

So the dog joined company with Greyskin, and they went on together towards Brussels. A little farther down the road they saw a cat sitting on the rubbish-heap outside a miserable hovel. The creature was half blind with age, and had a face as long as a fiddle.

"Why, what is the matter with you?" asked Greyskin, who had a tender heart.

"Matter enough," said the cat. "I've just been turned out of house and home, and all because I took a little piece of bacon from the larder. Upon my honour, it was no bigger than a baby's fist, but they made as much fuss as though it had been a whole gammon. I was beaten, and kicked out to starve. If I could catch mice as I used to do, it would not matter so much, but the mice are too quick for me nowadays. They laugh at me. Nothing remains for me but to die, and I hope it may be soon."

"Nonsense," said Greyskin. "You shall live to laugh at all your troubles. Come along with us and sing in the choir at St. Gudule. Your voice is a little too thin for my own taste, but you'll make a very good soprano in a trio. What do you say?"

"You give me new hopes," answered the cat. "Of course I'll join you," and so the three went on together.

Towards nightfall they arrived at a farmyard, on the gate of which a cock was crowing lustily.

"Hallo!" said Greyskin. "What's all this about?"

"I am singing my last song on earth," said the cock. "An hour ago I sang a song, although it is not my usual custom to crow in the afternoon, and as I ended I heard the farmer's wife say: 'Hearken to Chanticleer. He's crowing for fine weather to-morrow. I wonder if he'd crow so loudly if he knew that we had guests coming, and that he was going into the pot to make their soup!' She has a horrid laugh, that woman. I have always hated her!"

"They Laugh At Me"

"And do you mean to tell me," said Greyskin, "that you are going to stay here quite contentedly till they come to wring your neck?"

"What else can I do?" asked Chanticleer.

"Join us, and turn your talents to account. We are all beautiful singers and we are going to Brussels to offer ourselves as choristers at St. Gudule. We were a trio before. With you we shall be a quartet, and that's one better!"

Chanticleer was only too glad to find a means of escape, so he willingly joined the party, and they once more took the road. A little while afterwards they came to a thick wood, which was the haunt of a notorious band of robbers. There they decided to rest for the night, so Greyskin and the dog lay down beneath the shelter of a large beech-tree, while the cat climbed on to one of the branches, and Chanticleer perched himself at the very top. From this lofty post he could see over the whole wood, and it was not long before he espied a light twinkling among the trees not far away.

"What Else Can I Do?" Asked Chanticleer

"There must be a house of some sort over there," he said to his companions. "Shall we go and see? We may find something to eat."

"Or some straw to lie upon, at any rate," said Greyskin. "This damp ground gives me rheumatics in my old bones."

"I was just thinking the same thing," said the dog. "Let us go."

So the four choristers, led by the cock, walked in the direction from which the light came, and before long they found themselves in front of a little house, the windows of which were brilliantly lighted. In order to reach to the windows the animals made a tower of their bodies, with Greyskin at the bottom and Chanticleer at the top.

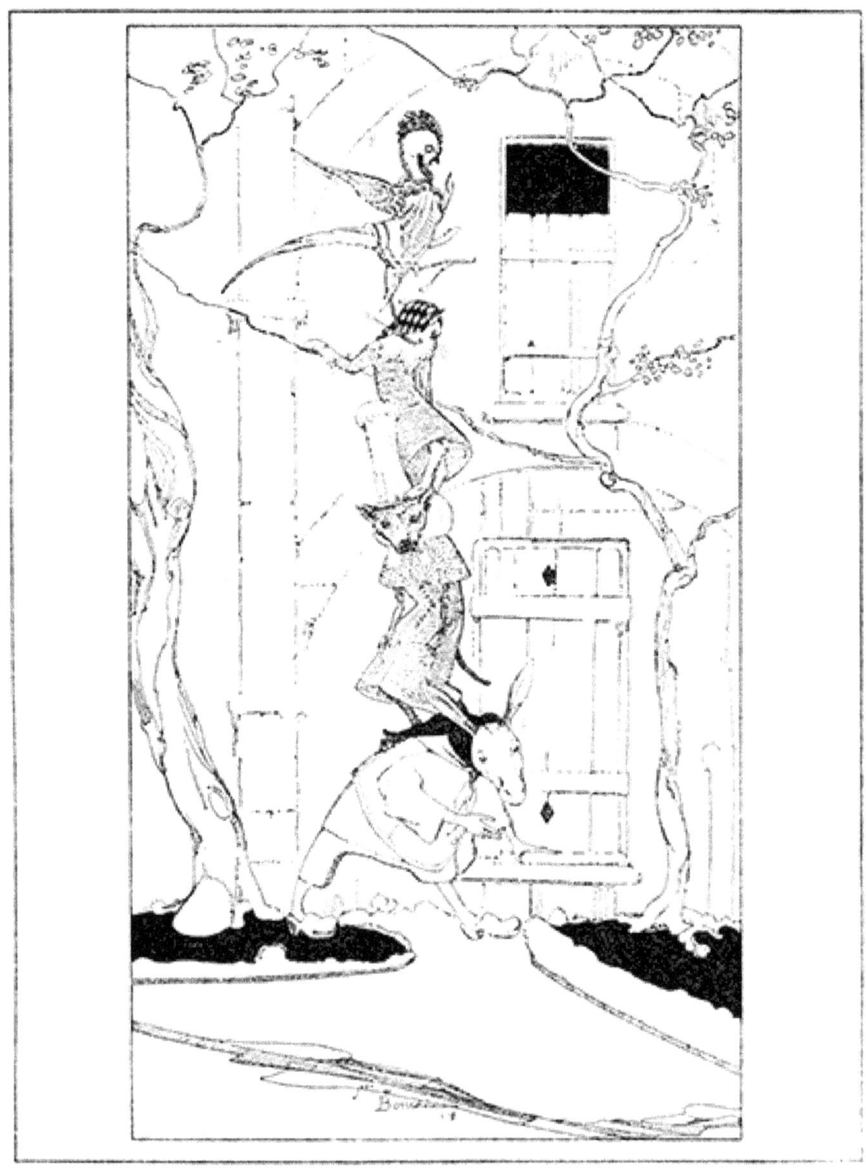

"Hush!" Said Chanticleer

Now this house was the abode of a band of robbers, who, at that very moment, were seated before a table laden with all kinds of food. There they sat and feasted, and poor Chanticleer's mouth watered as he watched them.

"Is there anybody inside?" asked the dog, who was impatient.

"Hush!" said Chanticleer. "Men! They're eating their dinner!"

"I wish I was," said the dog. "What are they eating?"

"All sorts of things—sausage, and fish...."

"Sausage!" said the dog.

"Fish!" said the cat.

"And ever so many other delicacies," Chanticleer went on. "Look here, friends. Wouldn't it be a fine thing if we could get a share of their meal? I confess that my stomach aches with hunger."

"And mine too," said the dog. "I've never been so hungry in my life. But how are we to get the food?"

"Let us serenade them, and perhaps they'll throw us something as a reward," said Greyskin. "Music, you know, has charms to soothe the savage breast."

This seemed such a good idea that the choristers lost no time in putting it into execution. All four began to sing. The donkey hee-hawed, the dog howled, the cat miaued, and the cock crowed. From the noise they made one would have thought that the heavens were falling.

Breaking The Glass To Smithereens

The effect of this marvellous quartet upon the robbers was instantaneous. Leaping from their seats, they ran from place to place in mortal terror, tumbling over one another, oversetting chairs and adding to the racket by their shrieks and cries. At that moment the cock fell against the window, breaking the glass to smithereens; the donkey gave the frame a push, and all the four precipitated themselves into the room. This was the last straw; the robbers could stand no more; half mad with fear they rushed to the door and fled into the forest.

Then our four choristers drew up to the table and set to work upon the food with which it was laden. Their long walk had given them a good appetite, so that there was little left by the time they had finished. Feeling drowsy after their meal, they then settled themselves to sleep. The donkey made himself a bed on a heap of straw in the yard; the dog stretched himself out upon the mat by the house door; the cat lay among the warm cinders on the hearth; and the cock perched upon the roof-top. A few minutes more and they were all fast asleep.

Meanwhile the robbers, who had retreated some distance into the forest, waited anxiously for something dreadful to happen. An hour passed by and there was neither sight nor sound to alarm them, so they began to feel a little ashamed of their cowardice. Creeping stealthily nearer to the cottage, they saw that everything was still, and that no light was showing from the windows.

At last the robber chief sent his lieutenant to spy out the land, and this man, returning to the cottage without mishap, found his way into the kitchen and proceeded to light a candle. He had no matches, but he saw two sparks of fire among the cinders on the hearth, so he went forward to get a light from them.

Now this light came from the cat's eyes, and as soon as puss felt the robber touch her, she sprang up, snarling and spitting, and scratched his face. With a scream of terror, he dropped his candle and rushed for the door, and as he passed the dog bit him in the leg. By this time the noise had awakened Greyskin, who got upon his feet just as the man ran by, and helped him forward with a mighty kick, which sent him flying out into the roadway. Seeing this, the cock on the housetop spread his wings and crowed in triumph, "Cock-a-doodle-doo!"

I wish you could have seen the way that robber ran! He covered the ground so quickly that he seemed like a flying shadow, and I am perfectly certain that not even a hare could have overtaken him. At last, panting for breath, he rejoined his comrades in the forest, who were eagerly awaiting his return.

"Well," cried the chief, "is the way clear? Can we go back?"

"Not on any account," cried the robber. "There's a horrible witch in the kitchen. Directly I entered she sprang at me and tore my face with her long claws, calling out at the same time to her creatures to come and devour me. As I ran through the door one of them buried his fangs in my leg, and a little farther on, in the yard, a great black monster struck at me with an enormous club, giving me a blow that nearly broke my back-bone. On the roof a little demon with wings and eyes that shone like coals of fire cried, 'Stop him! Eat him! Stop him! Eat him!' You may guess that I did not wait for more. It is a miracle that I have escaped with my life!"

When they heard this terrible story the robbers lost no time in decamping, and such was their terror that they deserted the forest altogether and went away to another part of the country. The result was that our four friends were left to dwell in the cottage, where they lived happily for the rest of their lives, and as they had now everything they wanted, they quite gave up their idea of going to St. Gudule.

The Robbers Lost No Time In Decamping

The King

THE TRIAL OF REYNARD THE FOX

I.
HOW CHANTICLEER THE COCK MADE COMPLAINT
AGAINST REYNARD

THERE was rejoicing among the animals, for it was said that Reynard the Fox—sly, spiteful Reynard—had at last repented him of his misdeeds and resolved to lead a new life. Such a thing was, indeed, very hard to believe, but nevertheless everybody said that it was true. Certainly he was seen no more in his usual haunts, or about the Court of King Lion. The news went round that he had put on the robe of piety and had become a hermit, endeavouring to atone, by fasting and prayer, for all the sins of which he had been guilty.

At the Court of King Nobel, Reynard's change of heart was the one topic of conversation. A few of the animals frankly expressed their doubts of the sincerity of such a tardy repentance, but the majority were quite willing to accept it, for, as a rule, one believes what one wishes to believe.

While the subject was still being eagerly discussed by the animals around the Lion's throne, the sound of wailing was heard, and a strange procession was seen making its way towards the King's throne. At the head of the procession marched Chanticleer the Cock, dressed in the deepest mourning and sobbing miserably, with bowed head. Behind him, borne by two hens, was a bier on which was stretched the headless body of a beautiful fowl, one of his daughters, and all the other hens of his family followed the bier, raising their voices to heaven in griev-ous lamentation. At this sad sight the whole Court stood in amaze, and many of the animals wept in sympathy with the bereaved father, who advanced towards the King's throne, crying for justice.

"Whom do you accuse?" asked the Lion.

"Whom should I accuse but that accursed Reynard, the source of untold mis-ery to me and mine? You know, O King, none better, how we have suffered from his cruelty in the past. The tale I now have to tell is a tale of wrong that would bring tears to the eyes of a stone image—a tale of treachery such as would abash the Evil One himself, a tale so base that I can hardly bring myself to utter it!"

"Say on," said the King, "and rest content, for if what you say be true, the Fox shall receive his due reward—I swear it by my crown!"

"Lord," continued Chanticleer, "I had six sons and fourteen daughters. We all dwelt together in the farmyard, a peaceable and happy family. The rigours of the winter were spent; spring had come again with its flowers and perfumes. The sun shone brightly, and insects abounded in the farmyard. We dwelt in the midst of abundance; we were happy, and as we thought, safe, for the farmer's six faithful dogs guarded us from danger. Alas, for our beautiful hopes! A few days ago Rey-nard appeared—cruel, black-hearted Reynard—and at one fell blow changed our happiness into misery.

"This is how it all happened, Sire. Reynard came to the farmyard one fine morning and brought me a letter bearing your Majesty's own seal. I opened it, and read that your Majesty had commanded that all the animals should hence-forward live together in peace. A noble ordinance, Sire, such as would make the world a beautiful place—were it not for villains. I gave the document back to Reynard, expressing my joy at the news it contained, whereupon he said: 'My heart is full, Cock, when I think of the cruelty with which I have treated you and your family in the past, but you need have no further fear, I have seen the error of my ways. Henceforth my life shall be given up to repentance and prayer. I have renounced all worldly pleasures. Even now I am on my way to a remote hermitage where, in fasting and solitude, I shall endeavour to atone for my sins.'

"Then the hypocritical wretch stretched his paw over my head and gave me his blessing and departed, reading his Book of Hours.

"Thinking no evil, and full of joy at the news, I called my children around me and cried: 'Rejoice, my dear ones. No more will you live in daily terror of your lives. Our noble King has given us his protection and has commanded the Fox to leave us alone. Reynard himself has just brought me the news, so I know it is true, and he himself has gone away to become a holy hermit!'

"My children danced with glee when they heard my words, and I danced with them, O King! We danced in the farmyard and in the garden, and in the kitchen garden, for it was as though a black cloud had vanished from over us.

At The Head Of The Procession Marched Chanticleer

"This was the very moment Reynard had been waiting for. He had not gone far away—no farther in fact than the shelter of the wall by the kitchen garden, and as soon as we reached there, he rushed out, fell upon the finest of my daughters and slew her before my eyes. It all happened in a flash! We ran hither and thither, trying to escape, but all in vain. Before we had gone a dozen steps the Fox was among us again, and killed fifteen of my children. Last night he returned, and slew her whose body now lies upon the bier. I have brought her here to show you, O King, that the sight of her corpse may strike pity into your heart, for I claim justice upon her murderer!"

So saying, the Cock bowed his head again and wept bitterly into his handkerchief, and pitiful sobs echoed from among the beasts around. Even the King could hardly restrain his emotion.

"A terrible tale, indeed," said he. "Our hearts are heavy for you, Cock, and it will go hard with this Reynard when he falls into our hands!" Then, addressing his courtiers, he asked for volunteers to go to the Fox's retreat and bring the murderer to justice. For a time there was no response, for few of the animals relished the task, but at last the Bear, who had an old grudge against Reynard, offered to go. "Leave this to me," said he. "If the Fox won't come quietly, I'll drag him here by his tail. He shall not escape!"

So the Bear set off to find Reynard, who had retreated to one of his châteaux—a veritable fortress—situated many miles away in the mountains at the very end of the kingdom. To reach it the Bear had to travel over lonely paths, and through dark woods, where he lost his way a hundred times, but at length he arrived at Reynard's house, only to find the massive door locked, and the walls so high that he could not climb them.

II.
HOW BRUIN THE BEAR WAS SENT TO BRING REYNARD TO COURT

"Open, in the name of the King!" cried Bruin, hammering at the door. "Come out, Reynard! I have been sent to bring you up for trial. You have come to the end of your rope at last! Open the door, I say, or I'll batter it down!"

From his safe retreat in the very heart of the fortress Reynard heard Bruin's clamour. He stretched himself lazily and yawned. "Now who is this pestilent fellow making such a din?" said he to his wife. "Well, I suppose I'd better go and see." So he made his way through the labyrinth of passages which led from his burrow to the open air, and peeped through the crack of the door. There was Bruin, hammering away at the massive oak, and roaring: "Come out, Reynard. Come out and be hanged!"

"What! is that you, Uncle Bruin?" said Reynard, opening the wicket. "You are in a noisy mood this morning. What is the matter?"

"The matter is that the King has sent me to bring you to Court," growled the Bear. "And you had best come quietly, for I represent the law."

"By all means," answered Reynard, opening the door. "My word, but I'm glad to see you, uncle! And an ambassador, too—such an honour! How are you, and what sort of a journey have you had? Very trying, I'm afraid. Really it was a shame to impose upon your good nature and send you all this way!"

The Fox's Château

So saying the Fox led the way into his castle, keeping up a continual patter of talk, so that Bruin could not get a word in edgeways.

"I'm so sorry to have kept you waiting at the gate," Reynard went on. "The fact is, I was dozing and did not hear you at first. I rarely sleep in the afternoon, but to-day I had such a heavy dinner that I felt extremely drowsy!"

"What did you have?" asked the Bear with interest.

"Oh, a simple meal enough. I am not rich, you know, and I have to eat what I can find. To-day it was a big comb of honey—not very much to my taste, but I was hungry and I ate it!"

Bruin pricked up his ears. "Eh?" said he. "Did you say honey?"

"Strange food for a fox, isn't it?" said Reynard. "I wish I hadn't touched the stuff now, for, to tell you the truth, it's lying on my chest like a load of lead. I swear never to eat it again, although I know a place, not far from here, where there are immense quantities of it!"

By this time Bruin was all agog with excitement.

"Nephew," said he, laying his paw on Reynard's shoulder, "show me the place where that honey is. My mouth is watering at the very thought of it. I love honey better than anything else in the world, and I'd give all I possess for a taste of it!"

"You are joking, no doubt," said Reynard laughingly. "How can any one like such stuff?"

"Joking, am I?" growled Bruin. "Just lead me to the honey and I'll show you whether I'm joking. I tell you I'd give my eyes and ears for a taste!"

"Well, if that's the case," said Reynard, "you shall be satisfied. There's a carpenter not far from here who keeps bees, and from time immemorial his family have been noted for the excellence of their honey. I'll take you there, and I'm very glad to be able to render you this little service. In return, all I ask of you is that you will speak up for me when I come before the King."

The Poor Beast Roared With Pain

"Of course I will," answered Bruin. "Let us go at once. I can hardly contain myself for impatience."

Reynard called upon Bruin to follow him and led the way to the carpenter's yard. The afternoon was very hot, and the carpenter was taking a nap after dinner. His yard was empty and in the middle of it was the trunk of a great oak-tree which he had laid out ready to be cut up into planks. The trunk was split down the middle, and kept open by two wedges of wood.

"Here you are!" said Reynard, going up to the tree-trunk. "This is the place where the carpenter keeps his honey. Put your muzzle in and root it out from the bottom. Don't eat too much!"

"Never fear," answered Bruin. "I'll be moderate." And he plunged his head and his two front paws into the crack. The next moment Reynard knocked out the wedges which kept the two halves of the trunk apart. They sprang together with the force of a steel spring, catching Bruin firmly by the nose and paws.

The poor beast roared with pain, making a din that echoed back like thunder from the mountains. The carpenter woke up from his slumber, and seizing an axe, ran out into the yard. His wife came tumbling out of the scullery with a broom in her hand, and people from the neighbouring village came running to see what all the noise was about. When they saw that the Bear was a prisoner they fell upon him and began to belabour him with mighty blows, while the unhappy creature gave himself up for lost. Maddened with pain, he redoubled his efforts to tear himself free, and at last succeeded in getting away, although he left most of the skin of his nose and paws behind. With the blood flowing from his muzzle, and his eyes shining red with rage, he made such a terrible picture that the people fled hither and thither, leaving him a free passage, and he limped off into the shelter of the woods, moaning and breathing out threats against his betrayer.

From a safe distance Reynard watched him go, with a malicious grin. "Farewell, Uncle Bear," said he. "I hope you found the honey good!"

III.
TYBERT'S MISSION AND HOW HE FARED

King Lion was furious when he saw the miserable state in which his ambassador returned. He immediately called a council of his ministers, to whom Bruin related all that had happened.

"This recreant must be punished," said the King when the tale was ended. "It is a disgrace to our kingdom that he remains at large. Somebody else must go to bring him here. Who shall it be?"

After a good deal of discussion it was decided that Tybert the Cat should undertake the task, for he was reputed to be as cunning and artful as Reynard himself. "Do not be deceived by his wiles," said the King. "No doubt he will try to flatter you, or to play upon your weaknesses, but pay no attention to his words. You must take this mission very seriously and not allow yourself to be led aside by anything. On your head be it!"

The Cat promised to be very circumspect, and set off at once. He travelled quickly, and soon arrived at the door of Reynard's castle, where he found the Fox playing with his cubs on the grass, tumbling them over and over, and having fine fun. It was a touching spectacle of domestic bliss. Reynard jumped to his feet when he saw Tybert.

"Why, cousin," said he, "this is a pleasant surprise! What makes you desert the gaieties of the Court for my poor home?"

"I come in the King's name," answered the Cat sternly. "He has sent me to bring you to Court, where you are to answer for your revolting crimes. The Bear returned yesterday, and the tale he told has stiffened the King's anger against you. I am to say that if you refuse to accompany me, your house shall be destroyed and your family wiped off the face of the earth!"

He Immediately Called A Council Of His Ministers

"Refuse," said Reynard, "whoever thought of refusing? I am sure the King has no more obedient subject than I. As for that Bruin, he is a bad subject, and I expect he has been telling a pack of lies about me. Do I look as if I could do anybody any harm? As a matter of fact I spend all my time here in meditation and prayer. But come in, come in! You must have a meal, for you have had a long journey. To-morrow we will set out together."

"It seems to me," said the Cat, "that it would be better if we started at once."

"Nonsense, my dear fellow," said Reynard. "It is bad to make a journey on an empty stomach. What difference will an hour or two make? We shall travel all the faster if we start in good condition."

"Well, there's something in that," said Tybert, who, to tell the truth, was not sorry of an excuse to break a fast of many hours. "What have you got for dinner?"

"What would you like?" asked Reynard. "Shall we say a comb of honey?"

"Bah!" cried the Cat. "Honey indeed! I loathe the stuff. Now if you had a nice fat mouse...!"

"Happy thought," said Reynard. "As it happens, I know a house close by where there are hundreds of mice, the fattest and sleekest creatures you ever saw in your life, and so tame that one can literally scoop them up by the score. I often catch a few myself when I am hungry and other game is scarce."

"Take Me To This House"

"Take me to this house," said Tybert. "Tame or not, I'll catch the mice if they are there. I love the creatures." And he licked his lips and stretched out his paws.

Now Reynard had spoken the truth when he said that he knew a house where mice abounded, and it was true also that he often went there—not in search of mice, but of chickens. The last time he had paid a visit he had found that the farmer had put a string noose over the hole by which he was used to enter, but fortunately for himself Reynard had discovered it in time.

Towards this house he now led the unsuspecting Tybert, and having shown him the hole, bade him enter and take his fill of the mice. Tybert obeyed, but no sooner had he got his head through the hole than the trap was sprung, and there he was, caught. He gave a scream of pain and fear, and from behind Reynard answered mockingly: "Sing away, cousin. I love to hear your voice. But mind you don't frighten the mice!" Then he took to his heels and ran back to his castle.

A minute or two later the farmer, having heard the Cat's miaulings, arrived armed with a heavy stick. "Ah, you thief," he cried, "I've got you at last, have I?" And he began to lay the stick on the Cat's back with all his might. Tybert kicked and struggled, and managed at last to get free, but he was more dead than alive when he went limping back to the King's Court.

IV.
HOW BLAIREAU THE BADGER BROUGHT REYNARD TO TRIAL

"This is monstrous," said King Nobel when he had heard Tybert's piteous tale. "It is no use paltering any longer. We must burn this caitiff's castle about his ears."

"One moment, Sire," said Blaireau the Badger, who was a great friend of Reynard's. "Our ancient laws demand that any person accused of crime shall be called three times before extreme measures are taken against him. Now Reynard has only been called twice. I propose, therefore, that he be given one more chance to render himself peacefully before your Majesty, and to defend himself. There are two sides to every story, and so far we have only heard one."

"That is all very well," said the King, "but who will be the messenger? It seems to me that the experiences of the other two will be little encouragement for a third."

"If no one else will go," answered Blaireau, "I will go myself. Reynard has been a very good friend of mine in the past, and I may be able to appeal to his better self."

"I doubt it," said the King; "but go by all means, and bring him back if you can. Should you fail, I will batter down his castle stone by stone."

So Blaireau went off on his mission, and arriving at the château, found Reynard in the midst of his family.

"Look here, uncle," said he, "there must be an end to all nonsense. The King is at the end of his patience, and unless you obey his commands he is determined to stick at nothing with you. Tybert and Bruin are both badly knocked about, and the sympathy of all the animals is with them. But for my pleadings the King would have sent an army to burn your castle about your ears. Be sensible now, and come back quietly with me. You have wits enough to defend yourself against all accusations and need not fear the issue. I tell you frankly, delay will be dangerous."

"Tybert And Bruin Are Badly Knocked About"

"Ah," said Reynard, "if those others had only spoken to me as you have spoken, my dear nephew, things would have been very different. They were insolent and they paid the price, but nobody shall say that Reynard the Fox was impervious to good counsel. Of course I will go with you—the sooner the better. I have no fear of being able to silence my calumniators. The King can't live without me—he knows it very well, and that fact alone will provide him with a good motive for giving me a free pardon."

Then Reynard took a tender farewell of Hermeline, his wife, and Reynkin, his eldest son, and all the other children, and set off with Blaireau towards the King's Court.

On the way Reynard said: "My dear Blaireau, this is a very solemn moment of my life! I cannot help feeling that I have not, perhaps, always lived as righteously as I might have done. It will relieve my mind somewhat if I might make confession of some of the most heinous of my crimes. Will you hear me?"

"And Caused Him To Jump At Least Twenty Feet Into The Air"

"Certainly," answered Blaireau. "I am glad to hear you have a contrite heart, uncle. Speak on by all means. Confession is the first step towards repentance."

"I have been a sad sinner," Reynard went on. "My heart fails me when I think of all the misery I have caused! I weep for the poor Bear, whose nose and paws are skinless because of me, and for the Cat, who suffered a terrible beating at the hands of the farmer. Then there was the Wolf—did I ever tell you about the Wolf?"

"No," said Blaireau, "you did not."

"Well," continued Reynard, "the Wolf and I were one day walking along the road when we came to a monastery. It was the time of evensong, and the sound of the bells made such a sweet music in the air that I felt my soul grow full of enthusiasm. 'Ah,' said I, 'if I were only one of the monks in that monastery, with what joy would I sound the bells!' Isengrim thought the idea a splendid one, and wished to carry it into practice, so, as he was not a monk, I took it upon myself to introduce him into the monastery at dead of night. There I tied him to the bell-rope and bade him pull, for the good of his soul. He pulled—ah, nephew, how enthusiastically he pulled! The bells rang as they had never rung before, and all the monks in the monastery came running to see what was the matter. Isengrim would have run away if he could, but alas, I had tied him so firmly to the rope that he could not escape, and he got a sound beating for his pains.

"Another time, still under the influence of his monastic ideas, Isengrim proposed to me that I should shave his head. I agreed, and when I had him in the chair, to my eternal shame be it said, I planted a burning firebrand on his pate, and caused him to jump at least twenty feet into the air. Ah, I am a miserable sinner." And Reynard broke into sobs and lamentations.

"Never mind," said Blaireau consolingly, "since you are truly repentant, all will be forgiven you. See, there are the towers of the King's palace. We shall soon be there. Get ready to make your speech of defence, for you will need all your eloquence this day."

V.

HOW REYNARD TOLD THE KING OF A HIDDEN TREASURE

When Reynard arrived at the court he found all the animals assembled to witness his trial. King Nobel sat on his throne, with the Queen by his side, and very cold and stern was the glance which the monarch cast upon Master Fox as he stepped up and made his obeisance. "Reynard," said the King, "you have been accused of crimes so many and so grievous that if only the half of all the accusations are true, you have merited death a hundred times. What have you to say?"

Reynard put a paw up to his face and brushed away a tear; then, with his voice broken with emotion, he answered: "My lord the King, I have been a miserable sinner, and there is nothing left for me to do but to cast myself upon your royal mercy. Where King Nobel sits, there justice and mercy sit also. I am sure of the one; therefore I make bold to plead earnestly for the other. Perhaps, O King, I am not so bad as I have been painted. The tongues of enemies have uttered slanders before to-day, and brought upright men to ruin. All I ask, O King, is that you will let me state my case, and, when I shall have finished my tale, judge me according to my deserts. I will keep nothing back, for in this serious hour I wish to speak nothing but the naked truth. Listen to me, O King, and let these others listen also. Perchance the sad story of my wrongdoings, and of my gradual fall from righteousness, may be a lesson to many here, and by serving as an example help to keep them upon the strait and narrow path."

"You have a glib tongue, Reynard," said the King. "It has saved you before to-day, but this time the count is too serious to be hidden by a mist of words. Yet speak on. The accused has a right to make his own defence, and that right I should be the last to deny, even to one forsworn and treacherous, as you have proved yourself to be."

Reynard sobbed aloud. "Hard words, O King," said he, "and harder still because of the truth that is in them. I do not complain. Meekly I bow the head and make confession of my sins."

At this all the animals settled themselves comfortably to listen. The idea of Reynard the Fox confessing anything was so new that not one of them would willingly have missed a word. Those of the animals who knew Reynard well regarded him a little uneasily, but nobody broke silence. Reynard remained for a time sobbing quietly with head bowed upon his paws, then, in a broken voice, he began to speak:

"I Was Mischievous And Unruly"

"From my very earliest years, O King," said he, "I was mischievous and unruly. Had there been anybody to give me counsel and guidance I might perhaps have outgrown the errors of my youth and become a worthy subject. Unfortunately I fell into bad company, and, under the influence of evil companions went rapidly from bad to worse. Isengrim the Wolf was my friend in those early days. He it was who taught me to steal and to prey upon the defenceless creatures of the woods and fields. My first victim, I well remember, was a young lamb which had strayed from the fold. Isengrim led me to her and persuaded me to kill her, and afterwards, in the same way, a goat and two young deer fell victims to my raging thirst for blood. Soon not a hen-house, not a fold was safe from my depredations. I killed for the sake of killing, and that part of the meat which I could not devour I gave to the Wolf, who was only too willing to take it, or hid it in certain holes and crannies in the wood."

All the time that Reynard had been speaking Isengrim had been making frantic efforts to speak, but a glance from the King had kept him silent. Now he could contain himself no longer. Trembling with fury, he rose to his feet and cried: "Lies! All lies, O King! Will your Majesty believe anything it pleases this slanderous dog to say?"

"Silence!" cried the King. "Your turn will come later. For the present let the accused speak without interruption!"

"Thanks, O King," said Reynard. "I can well understand the Wolf's wrath when his connexion with so vile a creature as I is thus brought to light. Yet I have sworn to tell the truth, and the truth I will tell without regard to persons. Sorry as I am to say it, the Wolf was not the only one to lead me into bad ways. Among my companions of those early days were also the Bear and the Cat. They made me hunt for them when I was young, and such was their voracity that there was little left for myself, and I should have died of hunger were it not for the fact that I was fortunate enough to discover a hidden treasure!"

"Eh, what's that?" said the King. "Did you say a treasure?"

"Aye," answered Reynard, "a treasure of gold, my lord; so great a treasure that it would take your servants many days even to count it all. And not gold alone, but precious gems—diamonds of the purest water, rubies red as blood, and emeralds green as the sea when the sun shines upon it!"

The Queen leaned forward upon her throne and fixed Reynard with burning eyes. "And pearls too?" she whispered.

"Pearls too, O Queen. Ropes of pearls that well would adorn your Majesty's fair neck. And jewelled crowns worthy of a royal brow! Hidden deep in the earth they lie, all those riches, and now they will lie there for ever, for nobody knows of them but myself. Perhaps it is as well. The lust of gold is the motive of many crimes, and this treasure has already been the cause of a serious attempt against the throne and the life of the King! But all this has nothing to do with my confession. With your Majesty's leave I will go on with what I was about to say."

The Trial Of Reynard The Fox

"One moment," said the Queen. "Those crowns you spoke of—describe them more fully. What stones had they, and how set?"

"Time enough for that," cried the King. "You shall try the crowns upon your head before all is done. Let the Fox tell us where this treasure is hidden; that is the important thing!"

"I had thought to carry the secret with me to the grave," said Reynard, "but in this solemn hour I can hide nothing. If it is your Majesty's will, I will tell all."

"And Pearls Too?" She Whispered

"Beware, O King!" cried the Bear. "He will deceive you now as he has deceived others. Believe not his lying words!"

"Silence!" cried the King. "This matter concerns me, and me alone. Let Reynard speak!"

Reynard cast a look of triumph at Bruin and Isengrim, and, smiling faintly, went on with his tale.

"The treasure was discovered first of all by my father. He came upon it one day when he was hunting in the forest, among the ruins of a palace that once belonged to an ancient king. There, in a deep hole, under a big stone, he found the gold and gems, and for ever afterwards he was a changed creature. No longer blithe and care-free, he slunk about as though overburdened with responsibility. He knew himself rich beyond compare—richer than any king in all the world, and gradually into his heart there crept the desire to win, by means of his riches, a place of power.

"At that time, O King, my father was bitter against your Majesty because of your disapproval of his manner of life, and I am sorry to say that he determined to wrest you from the throne and to set up another in your place. Full of this project, he took Tybert the Cat into his confidence. The two met together secretly in the forest of the Ardennes, and after much discussion they decided to offer the throne to Bruin the Bear!"

"Ah!" ejaculated the King, turning his gaze upon Bruin, who was too furious to speak. "So now we know why you wished to still Reynard's tongue."

"The Bear was delighted with the prospect," Reynard went on, "and strutted about the forest as though he were already crowned. He was always talking of the fine laws he would make and the splendid time he would have, but he was too stupid to be of much use as a plotter. Indeed, it was for reason of his stupidity that my father and Tybert chose him as king, for they thought they could make of him a useful tool. They had, however, to lay their plans without him, and the better to carry them out, they called Isengrim the Wolf, and Grimbard the Ape, into conference. The five met together at a certain place between Heyst and Gand, and it was there, O King, that your death was decided upon. Each of the conspirators took a solemn oath not to divulge the proceedings to a living soul, and having settled the very hour and day of your Majesty's assassination, they departed to their homes.

"Now, like all apes, Grimbard was a chatterer, and no sooner was he within his house than he told his wife all that had happened, explaining to her that it was a great secret and she was not to tell a soul. Of course she promised faithfully to keep a still tongue in her head, and as a matter of fact I believe she did manage to keep the secret for a whole day. Then she happened to meet my wife in the woods, and having sworn *her* to secrecy, told her the whole thing. My wife, out of a feeling of love and regard to your Majesty, thought it her duty to inform me, which she did, immediately she returned home, without keeping back a single detail.

"I could not believe my ears at first. 'What! Bruin, king!' I cried. 'That great fat lump of hairy stupidity, king of the animals! Is the world going mad? Would they dethrone our loved and gracious lord in favour of so base a beast?' There and then, O King, I raised my hand above my head and swore to defend your Majesty's life to the last. 'While Reynard lives,' I said, 'the King's throne shall be secure, cost what it may!'

"From that moment I thought of nothing else but how best to thwart my father's base plans. It seemed to me that if I could only discover the treasure I might stop the whole thing, for the conspirators relied upon the gold to pay the armies they intended to raise. For days, therefore, I lurked about the woods, following my father wherever he went, in the hope that, sooner or later, he would betray the treasure's whereabouts. But he was far too wary to go near it, and had it not been for the stupidity of the Ape I might have remained none the wiser. One day I noticed Grimbard wheeling a barrow through the forest with an air of great secrecy, and following him unseen, at a safe distance, I saw him stop in the midst of the ruins of that ancient palace in the forest. There, at the foot of a great tree, he lifted a heavy stone, discovering a deep hole, from which he took several vases filled to the brim with golden coins. These he placed upon his barrow, and having carefully covered up the hole again, trundled off into the forest.

"I Saw Him Stop At The Foot Of A Great Tree"

"No sooner had he disappeared amid the shade of the trees than I ran forward and lifted the stone. What a sight met my eyes! There lay the treasure—chest upon chest of shining gold, and heaps of jewels flashing with rays of many-coloured light. My eyes were nearly blinded by the splendour.

"Even as I stood gazing in a sort of dazed trance, I realized what I must do. If I could get this treasure away from the place where it was hidden, and, unknown to the conspirators, transport it somewhere else, their plot would be strangled at its birth. Unfortunately the treasure was heavy and I had no means of conveyance—

not even a barrow, but I took counsel of Hermeline, my wife, and she, noble soul as she is, strengthened me in my resolve. 'Though we wear our paws to the bone,' said she, 'we must take the treasure away and save the life of our noble and our beloved King.' That very night we began our task, and little by little we moved the treasure, hiding it in a safe place known only to ourselves. For the best part of a month we laboured, working only at night, and fearful every moment that we should be discovered. At last everything was finished, and the whole of the treasure removed.

The Conspiracy Gained Adherents Every Day

"In the meantime, the conspiracy gained adherents every day. My father was the life and soul of the plot. He sent messengers far and near, into every corner of the land, to win the animals over to his side. 'Those who enrol under my banner,' said he, 'shall receive a large sum of money paid in advance. I do not ask them to trust my word, but to come to me and let me pour the money into their hands.' In such circumstance what wonder that his supporters grew every hour. Before long he had gathered together an immense army, which was increased by troops raised by the Bear, the Wolf, and the Cat. Bruin, in particular, was very proud of his success in raising soldiers. He already fancied himself king, and walked about giving orders to everybody who crossed his path.

"Now the time for payment had come, so my father, accompanied by Grimbard and the Cat, made his way to the hiding-place of the treasure to bring out the gold. I watched them from afar, and saw them uncover the hole, and never to my dying day shall I forget the scream my father uttered when he saw that the treasure was no longer there. Frantically the two of them dug up the soil around the place in the hope that they were mistaken, but not a single gold piece could they find. At last Grimbard, chattering with fear, turned and slunk away, while my father crept home and hanged himself with a cord to a nail just outside the back door. A terrible end, O King, but though he was my father, I cannot help feeling he deserved the misery he had brought upon himself. As for Bruin, he found himself faced with the necessity of explaining to the soldiers that no money was forthcoming, and being a coward at heart, he shirked the task. He, too, fled secretly, and Tybert the Cat soon followed. To-day, sire, these three stand among the foremost of my accusers. If I have sinned, have they not sinned too, and in greater measure?"

The Suit Of Golden Armour Emrik Wore

The King waved his paw impatiently. "We will deal with them presently," said he. "For the present, keep to your tale. Where is the treasure hidden? Speak, and lie not, on your life!"

"Why should I lie, O King?" asked Reynard in an aggrieved tone. "Have I not sworn to tell the truth? In Western Flanders there is a little wood called Husterloo. In the midst of that wood lies a pool, which is known by the name of Krekelput.[1] It is a dreary place, O King, and solitary, for it lies among marshes where no man can pass. No sound is heard in that place save only the call of the carrion-crow by day, and the dismal hooting of the owl by night. There, close to that pool, I hid the treasure, in a hole in the earth which I covered with soil, marking the place with three great stones. Remove those stones, and dig up the soil, and you will discover three enormous golden vases, beautifully carved and modelled. In the first is the royal crown of the ancient King Emrik, which Bruin thought to wear. In the second is the crown of Emrik's queen—a thing of wonder, flashing with splendid gems; and in the third is the suit of golden armour Emrik wore. Beneath these three vases lies the rest of the treasure—chest after chest of golden coins, ropes of pearls, necklaces of diamonds and rubies, so many gems that I cannot describe them all. If your Majesty will send trusty messengers to Krekelput, they can easily prove the truth of what I say!"

During this recital the King had raised himself from his throne in his excitement, and now he turned to the assembled animals and cried: "Which of you knows Krekelput? Who will go and fetch the treasure?"

Nobody answered, for, as a matter of fact, not a soul present had ever heard of Krekelput before Reynard mentioned the name.

"Come, come," cried the King. "One of you must know the wood of Husterloo and the pool of which Reynard speaks!"

"Be patient with them, Sire," said Reynard. "They are afraid to speak. The Hare knows the place very well. Do you not remember, friend," said he, fixing the Hare with a menacing glance, "you took refuge in the wood of Husterloo one day when the hounds were after you!"

"I cannot remember very well," stammered the Hare, who was nearly out of his senses with fright. "Perhaps I did!"

"Of course you did," said Reynard, "and you could find the place again, no doubt?"

"I am not sure," said the poor Hare, who indeed had never heard of Husterloo.

"A truce to all this!" cried the King impatiently. "If you cannot remember, Reynard shall go with you to refresh your memory, and Bellyn the Ram shall accompany the two of you to see that you do not run away. Be off with you at once, and bring back the treasure as quickly as you can, for my eyes are aching for a sight of Emrik's crown and the suit of golden armour Emrik wore."

---

[1] Snail's well.

They Walked In Silence

"And forget not the ropes of pearls and the jewelled coronet!" cried the Queen. "Bring those first!"

"I will bring everything in good time," said Reynard; "trust me for that. But before I set out on this journey I must go to Rome to ask absolution of the Pope for all the sins I have committed. Suffer me first of all to go on this pilgrimage, O King, and, if you will, send Bellyn and the Hare with me to see that I do not escape.

Nothing is further from my thoughts, but after what has happened I cannot expect your Majesty to trust my word, and I am content to go in ward."

"Be it so!" said the King. "Set off at once and return as soon as may be. And now there is another little affair to settle! Where is Bruin, our would-be king. Stand forth, Bruin, with your precious conspirators, the Wolf, the Cat, and the Ape." But nobody answered, for seeing how affairs were going all the four had quietly slipped away, fearing to stay and face the vengeance of the King.

Reynard smiled maliciously as he put on a pilgrim's cloak and marched away with Bellyn and the Hare along the road that led from the Court.

For several miles they walked in silence. Then Reynard sighed and said: "Ah, friends, how I long to see my dear wife and children just once more before I go on this long journey that lies before us. Let us take the road that leads past my castle of Malpertuis. It is not much out of our way, and we can enter there and refresh ourselves."

The Hare was too frightened to dispute the matter, and Bellyn on his part good-humouredly agreed, so the three of them took the road to Malpertuis, and before long came to the gate of Reynard's castle.

Reynard Sprang At His Throat

"Here we are at last, Cousin Bellyn," said Reynard. "Did you ever see such fine pastures! You must be famished after our long tramp. Take a rest a while and eat some of this sweet grass, while I and the Hare go into the house and console my wife for the long separation that is before her. We shall not stay more than a few minutes."

"Well, hurry up," said Bellyn, who had already begun to graze. "I will wait for you, but don't stay talking all day!"

So Reynard and the Hare went into the house, where they were met by Hermeline, Reynard's devoted spouse.

"What, husband," said she, "are you back already? How did things go at Court?"

"Just as I said they would," answered Reynard. "When the King heard my tale he acquitted me of the charges that had been brought against me, and allowed me to return here in honour. The Wolf, the Bear, and the Cat, who were my most powerful enemies, have fled the Court, so that, for the time being, they have escaped my vengeance; but I have brought with me this fellow whom you see at my side, for he was among the foremost of my accusers!"

When he heard these words the poor Hare trembled with fright, and turned to flee, but in a moment Reynard sprang at his throat. One loud cry he gave for help, but Bellyn, peacefully cropping the grass outside, did not hear, and the next moment the Hare was dead. Then Reynard and Hermeline and all the little foxes had a splendid feast, and in less than half an hour nothing was left of the Hare's carcass but the head.

While they were still feasting there came a loud knocking at the door. It was Bellyn, who, having eaten his fill, was now impatient with waiting.

Snatching up the head of the Hare Reynard put it into a bag, which he carefully sealed. Then, running to the door, he threw it open.

"You have been a long time!" grumbled Bellyn. "Where is the Hare?"

"Oh, he is just inside, playing with my little ones," said Reynard. "He's a merry fellow, that one, and so fond of children that it is beautiful to watch him. Leave him alone for a time. He'll be out presently. While you are waiting, you might run back to the King with this bag, which he asked me to send him. It contains papers referring to the conspiracy—papers which involve a great many people at Court, in fact nearly all of the animals except yourself. Hurry off with it, and give it into the King's own hands, and, as you value your life, do not open the bag upon the road, or the King will suspect that you also are involved and have erased your name on the way."

"Did the King say I was to take back the papers?" asked Bellyn.

"Of course he did!" answered Reynard. "'Send them back by my trusty Bellyn'—those were his very words, and he whispered in my ear that you were the only one among the whole court that he could trust. I should not be surprised if he gave you a handsome reward, and perhaps made you a peer of the realm!"

"Give me the bag!" cried Bellyn. "I'll take it to the King. I shall not be long. Wait until I come back, and tell the Hare that he is on no account to set out without me."

"You Have Merited Death A Hundred Times"

"Never fear," said Reynard. "He'll not stir a step out of my castle—I'll answer for that. Farewell, good Bellyn. I will be waiting here when you return!"

Full of pride at his important mission, Bellyn trotted off down the road, bearing the bag very carefully with him, and Reynard, with a spiteful smile, stood and watched him till he was out of sight.

In good time Bellyn returned to the Court and handed to the astonished King the bag which Reynard had sent. The King broke the seal, and gazed inside, while the Queen pressed close to him, peering over his shoulder. The next moment he gave a cry of horror, as he drew forth the head of the poor Hare. The Queen fell to the ground in a dead faint, and for a time the King remained holding the head in his hands, gazing at it vacantly. Then he cast it from him, and without a word turned his steps towards his palace, where he immediately took to his bed, for the shock of the thing had made him ill. Not for several weeks afterwards, when he had somewhat recovered, was he able to turn his thoughts to vengeance. Then he gave orders for a large army to march to Reynard's castle of Malpertuis to raze it to the ground, and bring back the Fox in chains.

The army set out, but when they arrived at Malpertuis they found the birds had flown. Reynard and Hermeline and all the little foxes had left the country, and were never seen again.

Some people say that they took up their abode in a distant land, where Reynard soon began once more to play his old tricks, until the King of that land caught him one day red-handed, and hanged him on the nearest tree without giving him a chance to say a word. I do not know whether this story is true, although I hope it is. All that I can say for certain is that Reynard and his family were never seen in King Nobel's dominions from that day on.

The King Of That Land Caught Him

Calf And Goat

THE MAGIC CAP

THERE was once a poor countryman, of whom his neighbours said that he had no more wits than he was born with, and that was not many. He was, indeed a simple-minded fellow, and anybody could get the better of him. One day the countryman's wife said to him: "Jan, put on your best smock and your soundest clogs, and go to the market to try and sell our calf. She is a good calf and you ought to get at least a hundred francs for her."

Away went Jan, along the road to the market town, with the calf behind him. He felt quite glad to be out on this fine spring day, and he hummed a merry tune as he plodded along. Three students who were lounging at the door of an inn saw him pass, and, marking his air of simplicity, thought it would be good fun to play a joke upon him, so one of them went up to him and said:

"Good-morning, friend! How much are you asking for your goat?"

"Goat?" answered the peasant in surprise. "This is not a goat, but a calf!"

"Indeed!" said the student politely. "And who told you that?"

"It was my wife," answered the peasant. "'Jan,' she said, 'go to the market and try to sell our calf.' I am sure she said calf. I could not make a mistake about such a thing!"

"Your wife was playing a joke on you," said the student. "Anybody can see that is a goat. If you don't believe me, ask the next person you meet on the road." And he went off, laughing.

Jan continued his walk, a little troubled in his mind, and before very long he saw the second of the students coming towards him. "Stay a minute, sir," he cried. "Do you mind looking at this animal of mine and telling me what sort of a creature it is?"

"Why, a goat, of course," answered the student.

"You're wrong," said the peasant. "It's a calf. My wife says so, and she could not be mistaken!"

"Have it your own way!" replied the student, "but if you'll take my advice you won't pretend that animal is a calf when you get to the market, unless you want to be hooted out of the town!"

"Ah!" said Jan, and he went on his way, muttering to himself, and casting many a troubled glance at the innocent calf who ambled along peacefully behind him. "If it is a goat it ought to have horns," he said to himself. "And it hasn't got any horns. But if it is a calf it will have horns when it grows to be a cow. Perhaps it is a goat-calf. I wonder whether goat-calves have horns!" And he continued to puzzle his poor brains about the matter until he was suddenly interrupted by a shout from the side of the road. The shout came from the third student, who had been waiting for him.

"Hallo, you there!" cried the student. "How much do you want for your goat?"

"Goat? Goat?" murmured the peasant in dismay. "Here, take the thing. If it's a goat, I don't want it, for I was sent to market to sell a calf. You may have it for nothing—I'll make you a present of it!" And so saying, he pushed the cord into the student's hand. Then turning his back without another word, he retraced his steps towards his home.

"You Were Being Made A Fool Of"

When his wife heard what had happened she was furious. "You stupid lout!"

she cried, "could you not see that you were being made a fool of?" And she called him all the names she could lay her tongue to, until the poor fellow blushed and hung his head for shame. Her anger did not last long, however, for she was a good woman and she knew that her husband's simplicity was not his fault, but his misfortune. Fortunately, she had quite enough wits for them both, and instead of wasting more time in reproaches, she set to work to think how she might pay back the practical jokers in their own coin. It did not take her long to think of a plan, and as the first step towards carrying it out, she put on her bonnet and went off to the town, where she called at three inns, paying at each of them for a dinner for four persons, the dinner to be eaten on the next market day. Returning home, she explained the plan to her husband and gave him very exact instructions as to the part he was to play.

When the next market day came round Jan set off for the town, and by the door of the very first inn on the road he met the three students. They exchanged a sly smile when they saw him, and one of them said: "Good morning, good fellow. And how do you find yourself to-day? I notice that you have no goat with you this time."

"Ha, ha, ha!" laughed Jan, "that was a good joke you played on me, but I bear you no ill-will for it. Come in and drink a glass of wine. I'm in funds this morning and I'll willingly stand treat."

The students accepted Jan's offer with enthusiasm, for they belonged to that class of men who are always thirsty. Accordingly the four went into the tavern; and Jan called for wine. When the time came to pay for it, he called the serving-maid, and taking off his cap, spun it round three times on his finger. "Madam," said he, "everything is paid for, isn't it?"

"Yes, sir, and thank you very much," answered the serving-maid.

The three students watched this procedure with a good deal of surprise, but Jan carried off the whole affair as if it were the most natural thing in the world. "Now, my friends," said he, "the doctors say it is bad to drink on an empty stomach. What do you say to a good meal?"

"Excellent," cried the students.

"Very well then, come along with me to the next inn, and you shall have one."

Laughing in their sleeves at the peasant's simplicity, the students followed. Arrived at the inn, Jan ordered dinner for four, and a heap of good things were put upon the table. After the repast, he called the serving-maid to him, took off his cap as before, and twirled it round three times on his finger. "Now then," said he, "everything is paid for, isn't that so?"

"Certainly, sir," answered the serving-maid, "and I am very much obliged to you."

At this the three students opened their eyes even wider than before, but Jan took not the slightest notice of their astonishment.

"What do you say, friends," he asked, "shall we go on to the town together and wash the dinner down with a glass of ale apiece?"

Jan And The Three Students

"As many as you please," answered the students joyfully, and so they followed Jan to the town, where he entered a third tavern and ordered drinks all round. Then, taking off his cap once again, he twirled it round three times on his finger, and said to the innkeeper: "Everything is paid for, isn't it, my good man?"

"Certainly, sir," said the innkeeper, bowing.

But this was more than the curiosity of the students could stand.

"Look here, gossip," said one of them, "how is it that you are able to get food and drink for nothing everywhere you go, simply by twirling your cap in people's faces?"

"Oh, that's easily explained," answered Jan, "This cap of mine is a magic cap, which was left to me by my great-great-grandmother, who was a witch, so I have heard say. If I twirl it on my finger, and say, 'Everything is paid for,'—well, everything *is* paid for! You understand me?"

"Perfectly," said the student. "My faith, but that is a wonderful cap—the very thing to have when one goes a journey! Will you sell it to me?"

"How much will you give me for it?" asked Jan.

"Two hundred francs!"

"Nonsense! Do you think I am going to brave my wife's anger for a paltry two hundred francs?"

"Well then, three hundred."

"Not enough! My wife says it is worth a fortune."

"Four hundred."

Jan shook his head doubtfully, and, seeing his hesitation, the student cried:

"Come now, we'll give you five hundred, and not a penny more. You'd better accept, or you'll lose your chance."

"Well then, hand over the money. I don't know what my wife will say, but...."

"She'll give you a kiss for making such a splendid bargain," cried the student, pushing a bag of coins into Jan's hand and snatching the magic cap. "Hurry off home as fast as you can to tell her the good news!" Then the three went away, laughing, slapping each other on the back in their joy at having got the better of the simple peasant.

That afternoon the students, eager to take advantage of the qualities of the magic cap, invited about fifty of their friends to a splendid feast at the largest inn in the town. Everybody who was invited came, as you may imagine, and the resources of the innkeeper were taxed to the utmost to supply the hungry and thirsty crowd with all that they wanted. When the feast was ended, the student who had Jan's cap called the host, and twirling it three times round his finger, said: "Now, sir, everything is paid for, isn't it?"

"Paid for?" cried the innkeeper. "What do you mean? I've not seen the colour of your money yet."

At this reply the student's face fell, but one of his companions snatched the cap from his hands. "Idiot," said he, "you twirled the cap the wrong way! I was watching the peasant carefully, and he twisted it like this." So saying, he gave the cap a twirl and said: "Now then, my good sir, I think you will agree that everything is paid for."

"I don't know whether you are trying to play a joke on me?" answered the innkeeper grimly, "but your idea of humour is not mine. You had better pay up at once, before I call the police!"

"Here, let me try," cried the third; and in his turn he twirled the cap, and, fixing the host with his eye, repeated that everything was paid for.

Twirled The Cap Round Three Times On His Finger

At this the innkeeper flew into a passion, and made such a fuss that the room was in an uproar. It was only by promising to pay him at once that the innkeeper could be quietened down, and prevented from putting his threat of calling the police into execution. The banquet cost a good round sum, and as the three students had no money left, their invited guests were obliged to subscribe the money between them, which they did with much grumbling. Afterwards they took their three hosts outside and dipped them into the horse-trough to punish them for their bad taste in playing practical jokes on their friends.

And a few miles away, in their little cottage, Jan and his wife sat counting the five hundred francs he had got for his greasy old cap, which indeed had not been left him by his great-great-grandmother, but which was as old and ragged as though it had!

And Dipped Them Into The Horse-Trough

Jan And Jannette

Were Carried Safely Over To The Other Bank

SUGAR-CANDY HOUSE

JAN and Jannette were brother and sister. They lived near a big wood, and every day they used to go to play there, fishing for sticklebacks in the streams, and making necklaces of red berries. One day they wandered farther from their home than usual, and all of a sudden they came to a brook crossed by a pretty red bridge. On the other side of the bridge, half hidden among the trees, they espied the roofs of a little pink cottage, which, when they came closer, they found to be built entirely of sugar-candy! Here was a delightful find for a little boy and girl who loved sweetstuff! They lost no time in breaking off pieces of the roof and popping them into their mouths.

Now in that house there lived an old wolf whose name was Garon. He was paralysed in one leg, and could not run very fast, but in all other respects he was as fierce and strong as he had been in his youth. When he heard Jan and Jannette breaking off bits of his roof he growled out, "Who is touching my Sugar-Candy House?" Then he came limping out to see who it was, but by that time the children were safely hidden in the woods.

"Who dares to touch my Sugar-Candy House?" roared the wolf again.

Then Jan replied:

"It's the wind so mild,
It's the wind so mild,
That lovable child!"

This satisfied the old wolf, and back he went to his house, grumbling.

The next day Jan and Jannette once again crossed over the little red bridge, and broke some more candy from the wolf's house. Out came Garon again, bristling all over.

"Who is touching my Sugar-Candy House?" he roared.

And Jan and Jannette replied:

> *"It's the wind so mild,*
> *It's the wind so mild,*
> *That lovable child!"*

"Very well," said the wolf, and he went back again, but this time there was a gleam of suspicion in his eye.

The next day was stormy, and hardly had Jan and Jannette reached the Sugar-Candy House than the wolf came out, and surprised them in the very act of breaking a piece off his window-sill.

"Oho!" said he. "It was the wind so mild, was it? That lovable child, eh? Precious lovable children, I must say! Gr-r-r, I'll eat them up!" And he sprang at Jan and Jannette, who took to their heels and ran off as fast as their legs could carry them. Garon pursued them at a good speed in spite of his stiff paw, and although he never gained upon them, yet he kept them in sight, and refused to give up the chase. The children looked back once or twice, and saw that the wolf was still following them, but they were not very much afraid, because they were confident of their ability to outrun him.

All of a sudden they found their way barred by a river. There was no bridge across it, and the water was very deep. What were they to do? Nearer and nearer came the wolf!

In the middle of the river some ducks were swimming, and Jan called out to them: "Little ducks! Little ducks! Carry us over the river on your backs, for if you do not the wolf will get us!"

So the ducks came swimming up, and Jan and Jannette climbed each on to the back of one, and were carried safely over to the other bank.

Presently the wolf, in his turn, came to the river. He had seen how the children had managed to cross, and he roared out at the ducks in a terrible voice, "Come and carry me over, or I'll eat you all up!"

"Very well," answered the ducks, and they swam to the bank, and Garon balanced himself on four of them, one paw on the back of each. But they had no intention of carrying the wicked old wolf to the other side, for they did not love him or any of his tribe, and, moreover, they objected to his impolite way of asking a favour. So, at a given signal from the leader, all the ducks dived in midstream, and left old Garon struggling in the water. Three times he went down and three times he came up, but the fourth time he sank never to rise any more.

That was the end of old Garon, and a good job, too, say I. I don't know what became of his Sugar-Candy House, but I dare say, if you could find the wood, and the sun had not melted the candy, or the rain washed it away, you might break a bit of it off for yourselves.

'Gr-R-R, I'll Eat Them Up!'

Wolf's Head

Jaco Peter And His Friend

POOR PETER

THERE was once a man named Jaco Peter who was so poor that he had not two sous to rub together. His clothes were rags, his boots were shocking, and as for his house, it was nothing but a miserable hovel hardly fit for a dog. The only friend poor Peter had in the world was a big fox who was called Reynard the Red because of the colour of his hide.

One day as Poor Peter was walking along the road looking out for stray scraps of food which he could pick up for his dinner, whom should he meet but Reynard, who was going off to spy round a farmhouse where, he had been told, there were some fine fat chickens.

"How now, Peter," said Reynard, "you look very miserable to-day! What is the matter?"

"I have fallen on bad luck," answered Peter gloomily. "I have found nothing to-day but two cabbage-stalks and a half-gnawed bone, and to make matters worse, the bone has no marrow in it."

"Why do you eat such stuff?" asked Reynard disgustedly. "Look at me—I am just as poor as you, yet I live on the fat of the land! And how do I do it, Peter? Why, by using my wits! Cheer up, my friend, you shall be a man of fortune yet, for I'll take your case in hand myself!"

Reynard was as good as his word. The same day he called at the King's palace and asked if he might borrow a bushel measure. Such an unusual request from a fox caused some amazement and the matter was brought to the notice of the King himself, who sent for Reynard and asked him what he wanted with such a thing.

"The fact is," answered Reynard, "that a friend of mine, a certain Lord Jaco Peter, has come by a good deal of money, and he wishes to measure it."

"Very well," said the King, "you may take the measure, but I would like to have it back when you have done with it, if you do not mind."

Off went Reynard with the bushel basket, and the same night, having stuck a couple of sous to the bottom of it with a bit of grease, he sent it back with a message to say that it was not large enough, and might he have another? In reply, the King sent a two-bushel measure, and after a time Reynard sent this back also, with a request for a larger one still. "If I have to measure the money with a thing like this," said he, "I shall be a month over the task."

"That friend of yours must be an enormously wealthy man," said the King. "Let me see—what did you say his name was? Lord Jaco Peter? I do not seem to remember a lord of that name in my dominions!"

"He is a foreign noble," said Reynard glibly, "who has only lately arrived in this country. He will shortly be coming to pay his respects to your Majesty, for it is his intention to ask for the hand of the Princess, your daughter, in marriage."

"That is a thing one must consider," replied the King, "but in the meantime I will gladly give your noble friend an audience."

Away went Reynard in high feather and recounted to Poor Peter all that had happened. "The affair is as good as finished," said he, "you shall marry the Princess and sit at the King's right hand!"

Peter looked down at his clothes, which indeed, were too well ventilated to be quite seemly, and made a grimace. "A fine lord I shall look!" said he, "with my toes sticking out of my boots and holes in my breeches."

"Never mind about that," Reynard answered. "Just leave everything to me, and all be well."

The next day, when the time came for the pair to set out for the palace, Reynard said to his friend: "Now pay great attention to what I have to say. Close by the King's palace there is a big muddy puddle in the middle of the road. When you come to that puddle I want you to trip over yourself and fall plump into it. Don't let there be any half measures! Get right into the mud—wallow in it, and smear yourself from head to foot!"

"But why...?" asked Peter.

"Never mind about why. Do as I tell you!"

Poor Peter carried out his directions to the letter. When they reached the puddle he pretended to slip, and fell souse into it, covering himself with a thick layer of mud. At sight of the disaster Reynard began to cry out in dismay, and the guards at the King's palace, who had seen the accident, came running up to offer their aid.

"Smear Yourself From Head To Foot"

"Did you fall down?" asked one of them politely. Peter was wiping the mud out of his mouth and could not answer, but the fox cried: "Of course he has fallen down, oaf! Do you think he sat in the puddle for amusement. Don't stand gaping there, but run to the palace quickly, and borrow a change of clothes, for this is Lord Jaco Peter who is on his way to visit the King. And look you," he added, as the guards ran off, "see that you bring some robes worthy of my lord's great estate, or it will be the worse for you!"

Away went the guards, and told the King's Chamberlain about the catastrophe. A few minutes later they returned bearing with them a magnificent robe of cloth-of-gold, beautifully embroidered and sewn with precious stones. Then they led Peter to a chamber, where he bathed himself and donned his new finery. Unfortunately the Chamberlain had forgotten to send any shoes, so there was Peter with his toes sticking out of his boots under his magnificent gown.

"Never mind," said Reynard, "you must keep your feet out of sight," and he led him before the King, who was immensely taken with his appearance.

"Tell me," he said to Reynard, after greetings had been exchanged, "why does your friend keep staring at his clothes. One would think he was not used to them!"

Reynard Seized The Opportunity To Warn His Friend

Reynard smiled. "As a matter of fact, your Majesty," he answered, "he is not. This dress of his came out of your Majesty's wardrobe, for he had the ill-fortune to spoil his own on the way here, by falling into a puddle. The gown is good enough, as it goes, of course; but my friend is used to something far finer. I would wager a thousand crowns he is thinking this very moment that he has never been so poorly clad before in his life! Is it not so, my lord?" he added, turning to Peter.

Peter gave a grin and a nod of the head, and the affair passed without further comment, but on their way in to dinner Reynard seized the opportunity to warn his friend against further faults of deportment. But, as the saying goes, it is no use trying to make a silk purse out of a sow's ear, and no sooner were they seated at table, and Peter saw the magnificent golden dishes, the delicate cut glass, and the fine candlesticks, than he opened his eyes wide, and gave an exclamation of astonishment.

"What is the matter now?" asked the King, staring at him.

An Exclamation Of Astonishment

"I crave your Majesty's pardon," said Reynard. "My friend is a little overwhelmed, for your customs are new to him. In his own palace, you see, he is used to a certain degree of luxury—such a service of plate, for instance, as this on the table, would there only be found in the servant's quarters. Come, come, my lord," he added, clapping Peter on the shoulder, "it will do you good to live the simple life. Spartan fare, my lord, Spartan fare!"

Peter rolled his eyes and grinned again, before falling to, with a fairly good appetite, upon the rich food spread before him.

"This lord must certainly be of enormous wealth," thought the King. "True, he has certain curious tricks of manner, such as supping his gravy with a table-knife, but what does a little thing like that matter! In other countries, other ways! That is a very good proverb."

After dinner was over Reynard broached the matter of Peter's marriage with the King's daughter, and the King gave his consent. He begged Reynard and his friend to remain at the palace as his guests until the ceremony should take place, and apportioned to them a magnificent suite of rooms. A week later Peter and the Princess were married. The poor man could hardly believe his good luck as he stood before the altar dressed out in gorgeous robes. All he could do was to stare like one who is dazed, and Reynard had to nudge him from behind to get him to make the responses. After the wedding a splendid feast was held, to which all the greatest and wealthiest lords in the kingdom were invited, and then the King's carriages arrived to conduct the happy pair to Peter's castle.

Now what was to be done? Peter's castle was a broken-down hovel at the edge of the forest. He shivered with fear when he thought of what the Princess would say when she saw it, with its mud floor, and its furniture consisting of one chair with no back, one battered table, and a heap of brushwood covered with a ragged pallet which served as a bed. Could Reynard overcome this difficulty as he had overcome all the others?

Of course he could, and he did! Away went the coaches, with Reynard sitting proudly on the box of the foremost, and presently the whole cortège halted before the gates of an enchanted castle, which Reynard had borrowed from the fairies of the forest. There Lord Jaco Peter and his bride lived for many happy years. They had six children, three boys and three girls, and Reynard was the friend of them all.

Away Went The Coaches

"Oh Dear Me, That's Twice!"

THE PEASANT AND HIS ASS

THERE once lived a poor peasant. I do not know his name, but he earned a living by gathering dead wood in the forest, and he had a donkey who was no bigger ass than himself. Perhaps by this you will be able to recognize him.

One day the peasant hitched his donkey into the shafts of his little cart and went off as usual to the wood for his day's toil. Arrived there, he tied the donkey to a tree and then, by way of the cart, climbed the trunk in order to break off some dead branches which he had noticed above. As he sat there, legs astraddle on the branch, busily breaking away the dead wood, along through the forest came a lord dressed in fine clothes, with his manservant behind him.

"Hallo! my man," cried the lord, "if you don't come down from that tree pretty soon you'll get a tumble. The branch you are sitting on is cracked."

"Cracked, is it?" answered the peasant. "Well, so much the worse for me." And he went on calmly with his work.

The lord went away shrugging his shoulders at the peasant's stupidity; and, sure enough, before he had gone very far, *crack! crack!* the branch broke, and down fell the peasant to the foot of the tree, giving himself a fine blow on the nose, which immediately swelled almost to the size of a turnip.

"My word," muttered the peasant, tenderly feeling the sore place, "that man must have been a sorcerer! He can foretell the future! He said I'd fall and I certainly have fallen! I must run after him and ask him to tell me something else. This is a chance not to be missed!"

So off he ran as fast as his bruised limbs would allow, in pursuit of the lord, and presently came up with him. "Hi, sir, wait a minute!" he cried. "You told me the truth about the tree. The branch broke right enough and I fell on my nose. Won't you tell me something else?"

"Willingly," answered the lord, "and I hope this time that you will pay heed to what I say. Take care not to load your ass too heavily, for if you do so he will bray, and if he brays three times running I predict that you will suddenly die."

"Oh dear me!" sighed the peasant. "I am the most unfortunate of men. Each prediction about my future seems to be an unhappy one. Nevertheless, I am very much obliged to you, sir. Good day." And he took off his cap to the lord and bowed, and lurched off back to his tree.

For a long time he worked busily, and found so much wood that his little cart soon became full. Then he remembered what the lord had told him about loading his ass too heavily, but he was so avaricious that he could not make up his mind to stop. "One more branch won't make any difference," he kept on saying as he piled more and more wood into the cart. At last the poor donkey could stand no more and, lifting his head, he uttered a loud "Hee-haw!"

At this the peasant turned pale with fright. "Stop, stop, what are you doing?" he cried. "Oh, my dear little ass, I beg you not to bray again. I will not put another branch into the cart. We will go home straight away and you shall have carrots for supper!"

So saying, he climbed to his seat and shook the reins as a signal for departure. The donkey pulled and pulled, but not an inch would the cart budge, although he strained his muscles to the utmost. Finding all his efforts vain, he turned his head and once again gave utterance to a loud bray of protest.

"Oh, dear me, that's twice!" cried the peasant, jumping down from his perch. "If he brays once more I'm a dead man. Do you hear that, little ass? For goodness' sake, remain dumb until we reach home, and I'll help you pull the cart!" Freed of the peasant's weight, the load for a time was easier to pull, but at the end of another ten minutes the weight began to tell again. The ass stopped and brayed loudly for the third time.

"That's finished it!" cried the peasant. "I am dead!" And he fell flat to the ground.

Left to himself, the ass wandered slowly on, dragging the load behind him. Soon he came to the gates of the town, and the guard took him and put him into the pound. After a time, as nobody claimed him, he was sold.

Meanwhile the peasant lay where he had fallen. Presently a carriage drove up, and the coachman was forced to pull in his horses because of the body that lay stretched across the road.

"Come," he cried, thinking that the peasant was drunk, "rouse yourself, swill-tub! Get up, unless you want to be run over!"

"I can't get up!" moaned the peasant.

"Hallo My Man," Cried The Lord

"Why not?"

"Because I'm dead!"

"Dead, are you?" cried the coachman, jumping from his seat in anger. "Well I've something here that will bring you to life again!" And he took his whip and laid on to the peasant with such a will that in less than ten seconds the fellow was capering about all over the road. Having thus effectively brought the dead man to life, he remounted his box and drove off grumbling.

In the roadway the peasant continued to dance about until the pain of his beating had somewhat subsided. Then he looked around, and for the first time missed his donkey.

"I Can't Get Up, Because I'm Dead!"

"Dear, dear, dear!" he cried, "one trouble after another! When I was dead I wished I was alive; now I'm alive I wish I was dead again, for I'm sore all over, and I've lost my donkey. Whatever shall I do?" And, groaning and grumbling, he set off along the road in search of his beast.

After a time he came to the gates of the town, where a sentry was standing with his pike on his shoulder. "Good morning, good man," said the peasant. "Have you seen my little ass?"

"Your ass!" answered the sentry, smiling. "The only ass that has passed through these gates to-day is already become burgomaster!"

"What! Burgomaster!" cried the peasant. "My ass Burgomaster! Tell me quickly, where does he live? I must go to him at once!"

Hardly able to control his amusement, the sentry pointed out the way to the Burgomaster's house, and thither went the peasant in all haste. Arrived at the door, he sounded the great bell—*Darlindindin!*—and a maidservant appeared.

"Is the Burgomaster at home?" asked the peasant. Yes, he was at home, and the maidservant led the peasant to the room where he sat behind a big table loaded with documents.

"Good morning, Ass!" said the peasant, with a grin of delight that twisted his swollen and discoloured features.

"Eh! what, what!" stammered the Burgomaster, turning purple with anger.

"I beg your pardon," said the peasant, "I should have said, 'Good morning, Mr. Ass, Esquire,' for you have become a great man now, while I am still a poor woodcutter. I don't envy you your good fortune, I am sure, although your promotion has left me without a donkey. Since you have become such a great lord, won't you give me back the ten florins you cost me, so that I may buy another?"

At this the Burgomaster's rage exploded. Leaping over the table with one bound, he seized the hapless peasant by the collar of his coat, threw open the door, and, with one mighty kick, sent him sprawling from top to bottom of the stairs.

Sent Him Sprawling From Top To Bottom Of The Stairs

The Eagle And The Kinglet

THE KING OF THE BIRDS

AT one time the birds, like the four-footed animals, were ruled over by the lion, who is the King of the Beasts, but they grew discontented with his dominion and decided to have a king of their own. It was the eagle's idea: he thought of it one day when he was standing on the lofty crag by his nest, gazing out upon the plain below, and he saw the lion, no bigger than a mouse in appearance, slinking beside a dried-up stream. "Earth-bound creature!" thought the eagle scornfully. "Who are you to reign over us, who cleave the air with wings and fly in the face of the sun! He who is lordliest among the birds should rule the feathered creatures, and surely I am he!"

So thinking, the eagle spread his wings and soared high into the air, and then swooped suddenly down upon the lion, casting sand into his eyes with a harsh scream of defiance. Having thus relieved his feelings, he sent messengers near and far to assemble all the birds that he might unfold his plan to them.

Such a scurry of wings as there was when the birds came to answer the summons! The sky was black with them, so that the animals on the earth below, fearing a dreadful storm, took shelter in their caves and holes. From north, south, east, and west they came; over mountain, valley, and plain; birds of all sorts and sizes, from the little humming-bird to the condor and the vulture. The ostrich left the burning plains where he loves to roam, and flapping his ridiculous wing, for he could not fly, raced to the meeting-place. All those birds that dwell in the tropical forests, and flash from tree to tree like living jewels in the green twilight; the penguins and skua-gulls from the icy north; the cormorants and shags, and all the hosts of the birds of the sea — if I were to go on naming them I should fill every page of this book and never even begin my story. And as they flew each uttered his own cry, so that what with the calling and the screaming, the whistling, warbling, chirping, and chattering, the air was filled with a mighty sound that echoed to the very ends of the world.

When all the birds were duly assembled the eagle addressed them thus: "Listen, brothers," said he, "I have called you together in order that we may choose a king, for it is not fitting that the lion, that earth-bound creature, should continue to reign over the free company of the birds. We are distinguished from the beasts by our power of flight, and it therefore seems to me that the crown of sovereignty should be given to the one amongst us who possesses that power in the fullest degree. What do you say? Shall we test this matter, and let him who can fly nearest to the sun be king?"

A confused chorus of cries answered his question, one bird speaking against another.

"What is flight compared to song?" asked the nightingale. "Let the sweetest singer among us reign."

The canary and the throstle and the blackcap all agreed with the nightingale, but they were shouted down.

"Beauty, beauty!" cried the peacock. "That is the test! A king should be resplendent in gay robes!" And he spread his gorgeous tail.

"Aye, there speaks wisdom," gobbled the turkey, turning red in the face, and strutting up and down. "What do you say, brother," he asked the cock. "Shall we arrange it so?"

"A fig for gay feathers!" cackled the ostrich. "Is our king then only to be looked at, or is he to do nothing all day but chirp and twitter foolish songs? As for flying, I found my wings of so little use that I gave up using them long ago. My idea is that we should settle this matter by a running race!"

And so the birds went on quarrelling and disputing until at last the eagle called for silence, and, addressing the company again, insisted upon the adoption of his own plan. He spoke sternly and menacingly, and as all the birds went in fear of his curved beak and sharp talons, no further objections were raised.

It was agreed that the trial should take place at once, and the cock was chosen to give the signal for the start. Very proud of the honour, he stationed himself on a little grassy knoll, and having ascertained that everybody was ready, gave a loud and clarion call. There was the sound as of a rushing mighty wind as all the birds sprang into the air. Only the eagle remained in his place, looking after the others a little contemptuously. So confident did he feel in his ability to outfly them all, that he allowed them at least five minutes start. Then, very leisurely, he spread his wings and soared. Up, up, up he went; he overtook the stragglers on the fringe of the crowd, passed through the thickest press, outdistanced the foremost flyer of them all. Still up and up he soared, exalting in his strength and power, until the birds flying far below were hidden by the clouds. Then he hung for a moment, motionless on extended wings, for he was a little wearied by his efforts.

"Is Our King Then Only To Be Looked At?"

All of a sudden he heard, above his head, a tiny *twit, twit, twit,* and looking up, saw, to his surprise, the golden-crested wren, one of the smallest of the birds, flying merrily above him.

"I have outdistanced you. I am king! I am king!" cried the wren in his joy.

"We will see," said the eagle grimly; and once again he beat his mighty wings and soared.

At the end of a further five minutes, he stopped again, only to hear, as before, the wren's cheerful twitter above him. Again and again the same thing happened. Try as he might, the eagle could not outdistance the tiny bird, and at last, worn out with his exertions, he was obliged to give up the contest, and to descend, crestfallen, to the earth again.

Birds Going To The Race

And how did the little wren, which is certainly not famed for its powers of flight, come to be able to defeat the mighty eagle? By a very simple trick! When the eagle started on its flight the wren was safely perched upon his back. There he clung until the eagle stopped flying, when it was an easy matter to rise from his place and fly a yard or two higher. When the eagle began to fly again, the wren again took its place on his back, and this continued time after time until the great bird was exhausted.

There Was The Sound As Of A Rushing Mighty Wind

Although nobody suspected the trick which the wren had played, the other birds were very indignant when they heard the wren declare that he had won the contest. "You, king!" they cried. "An insignificant thing like you! It would be a disgrace to us if we were to suffer it. We would rather be ruled by the lion! At any rate, he had majesty of deportment and dignity. You have neither grace nor wisdom, strength nor beauty. Away with you before we tear you to pieces!"

The wren was as perky as you please, and for only answer he flew to the boughs of a tree, whence he looked down on them all with his head on one side, chirping, "I am king! I am king. Bow down and make obeisance!"

A great cry of anger arose. "Kill him! Kill him!" screamed the hawk. "Tear him to pieces!"

"You will have to catch him first!" twittered the wren, and as the hawk made a rush at him, he popped into a hole in the trunk of a tree—a hole so small that nobody could get at him. From the shelter of that safe retreat he continued to gibe at the birds, issuing commands, and asserting that he was their king.

What was to be done? Nobody could get at the wren, and yet all the birds felt that he should be punished for his impudence. A consultation was held, and it was finally decided to set the owl as a guard at the mouth of his hole. "Sooner or later," said the eagle, "he will have to come out in order to get food, and then we will have him. If, however, he elects to stay where he is, let him; either way our purpose will be served."

So the owl mounted guard by the hole in the trunk of the tree, and having given him the most careful instructions not on any account to let the wren escape, the other birds flew away. All that day the owl remained vigilant at his post, and though the wren put his head out of the hole a hundred times, he always found his guard keeping careful watch. Night fell, and a great silence fell upon the woods, but still the owl kept awake for hour after hour, watching with unwinking eyes. At last, towards morning, his vigilance relaxed a little. His head sank forward on his breast; and he fell fast asleep. Hardly had his eyes closed than, *rip!* the wren darted out of his hole, and the next moment he had vanished among the trees.

When the birds returned the next morning they were furious to find that their prisoner had escaped. "Unfaithful servant," they cried, "you have betrayed your trust!" And they fell upon the owl to put him to death. With some difficulty he managed to escape, but ever since that time the birds chase the owl wherever they see him, for they are still angry with him. To keep out of their way he has to hide during the day and venture out only at night, when all the other birds are fast asleep.

As for the golden-crested wren, he is known as the Kinglet, or little king, to this day.

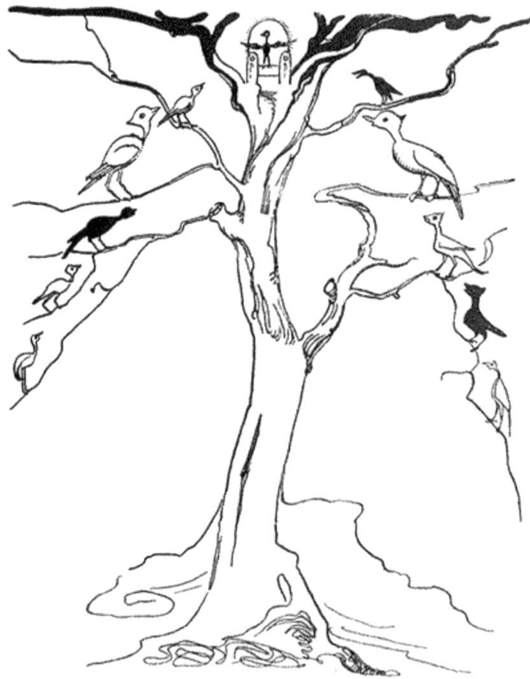

He Is Known As The Kinglet

Donatus

A DRUM FULL OF BEES

A CERTAIN regiment had for its drummer an old man named Donatus. He was a good-for-nothing rascal, who spent most of his time in the tavern drinking and playing cards, but he was an excellent drummer for all that, and it was a fine sight to see him on parade days, marching along with the band, and playing on his drum with a flourish that was the envy of all the boys in the town. None of his companions in the regiment liked Donatus, because of his fondness for playing practical jokes. There was hardly one of them whom at some time or another he had not hoaxed, and as most of his jokes were spiteful ones, nobody pretended to be sorry when one day the drummer was found cheating at cards, and being brought before the Captain, was dismissed from the regiment. It was in vain that he pleaded for mercy, with the tears running down his face. The Captain had forgiven him many times, and was determined not to do so again.

"Well," said Donatus at last, "if I must go, I beg you, Captain, to let me keep my drum. I have played on it since I was a lad of fourteen, and I know no other trade. If you take it away from me, I don't know how I am going to live, but with it I may perhaps manage to turn an honest penny or two."

"Very well, you old scoundrel," answered the Captain. "Keep your drum and take yourself off; only be quick about it, or you shall be soundly thrashed."

So away went Donatus with his drum on his back, and not having any particular place to go to, he just took the first road that came, and marched along it all day until he was forced to rest because his legs were so tired. Setting his drum down in the middle of the road he sat upon it and began to wonder what he should do for food and a bed for the night. First of all he turned out his pockets to see what he could find, but there was nothing there except two sous and a pack of very greasy playing cards. Donatus put them back again, with a sigh, and fell again to wondering how he was going to fare.

Now the road along which he had been walking was bordered by a dense forest, and suddenly Donatus thought that if he were to get among the trees he could at least find shelter. So he shouldered his drum again and entered the wood. Hardly had he done so than he heard a loud humming noise, and proceeding in the direction from which it came, he saw a swarm of bees hanging to the branch of a big tree.

"Here's fine fruit!" said he to himself, laughing. "I'll pluck them. They may come in useful one of these days!" So he took off the top skin of his drum, and having skilfully caused the swarm to drop inside the instrument, replaced the skin and went on his way.

Presently he came to a little house in the wood, and knocked at the door to ask for shelter for the night. The door was opened by a peasant woman of comely appearance, but with a very disagreeable expression of face. She looked the drummer up and down very sourly. "Be off with you!" she said, "we want no soldiers here. We have seen your kind before, my man, and do not like them." And so saying, she very rudely shut the door in his face.

"Now what am I to do?" thought Donatus ruefully. "Night has fallen, and I am too weary to wander any farther. A plague take that hard-hearted vixen, who will not take pity on my misfortunes!"

Thus reflecting, he cast his eye about to look for a corner in which he might rest, and suddenly spied a heap of faggots piled up against the cottage wall. Climbing to the top of the heap, he found that it was possible to reach the window of the attic, which fortunately stood open, so he lost no time in crawling inside, where he stretched himself out upon the planks to sleep.

Now the attic happened to be directly above the kitchen, and as there was a knot-hole in the wooden floor, the drummer could see everything that was going on in the room below. There was the peasant-woman busily preparing the supper, and the fragrant fumes which rose from the viands tickled the drummer's nose, and made the water run out of the corners of his mouth.

After a time there was a loud knock at the house door, and the woman hurried to open it, admitting a man dressed in a long cloak. He was the village beadle, and a nephew of the woman's husband, but that good man had such a hatred of beadles that he could not bear to look at one, and his nephew never dared to come to the house while the husband was at home. His visits therefore were few and far between, but when he did come his aunt always feasted him right royally. This time she bade him welcome with great tenderness, helped him off with his cloak and sat him down at the table, upon which she placed a fine roast fowl, with a gammon of bacon and a bottle of wine.

"Ha, ha!" cried the beadle, rubbing his hands. "You are a famous hostess, aunt! My walk has given me an appetite, and I am just in a condition to do justice to your good victuals. Here's health!" And he filled a glass with wine and drained it to the dregs.

There Was A Knot-Hole In The Wooden Floor

"Gr-r, you greedy fellow!" muttered the drummer, who was lying full length in the attic above with his eye to the knot-hole. "I hope it may choke you!" And he watched eagerly while the beadle began to fall to upon the roast fowl.

Suddenly the feast was interrupted by another loud knock at the door.

"My husband!" cried the woman in great agitation. "He has come back unexpectedly. If he finds you here, something terrible will happen, for he cannot bear the sight of a beadle. Quick! jump into this chest and pull down the lid, while I clear away all signs of the supper!"

The beadle, who was just as frightened as his hostess, lost no time in doing as she bade him. He hopped into the chest and pulled down the lid, while she hurried to clear the table. All this time the husband was thundering at the door, very impatient at being kept waiting. When at last his wife let him in, he flew into a temper and began to scold her.

"I am very sorry, good man," she answered, "but I did not hear you knock, I was hard at work in the scullery."

"Bring me something to eat!" growled the man.

"Just as you like," answered his wife. "But if I were you I would not sup so late—you know how it always gives you indigestion. Wouldn't it be better to go straight to bed?"

"Hold your peace, woman," said her spouse. "I am not sleepy!" And he sat himself down at the table.

Hardly had he done so than there came a loud knocking on the floor of the attic above his head.

"What is that?" he cried, jumping up. "Is there somebody in the attic?"

"Not that I know of," answered his wife. "Nobody has been here all day except a soldier with a most villainous face, who came begging. I sent him away with a flea in his ear, I assure you."

"Did you so?" said her husband. "Well, I believe he has managed to get into the attic. I remember now that I forgot to fasten the window." Off he went upstairs to see, and sure enough, there was the drummer, who was not slow in explaining his presence.

"Well, come along downstairs and warm yourself," said the peasant. "My wife is just about to get my supper, and I expect there will be enough for two."

Nothing loath, the drummer accompanied his host to the kitchen, and sat down at the table, paying no heed to the venomous glances which the woman of the house cast at him as she slammed down a loaf of black bread and a bowl of milk.

"Ho, ho," said the drummer to himself. "There is fowl for the beadle and dry bread for the good man and his guest. Well, we shall see!" And he gave a kick with his foot to the drum which was under the table.

"What have you there?" asked the peasant, starting up at the sound.

"Oh, that is my oracle," answered the drummer coolly.

"Your oracle! Does he, then, speak to you?"

"Certainly," answered the drummer. "He speaks to me three times a day."

"Faith," said the peasant, "I should very much like to hear him."

So the drummer picked up his drumsticks and beat a lively tattoo upon the drum, and, aroused by the noise and vibration, the swarm of bees within began to buzz about in great commotion.

"Wonderful! Wonderful!" cried the peasant delightedly, as he listened to the humming. "And do you really understand that language? What does the oracle say?"

"I Did Not Hear You Knock"

"He says," answered the peasant, "that there is no need for us to drink sour milk, because there is a bottle of wine standing by the wall, just behind the big chest."

"Ha, ha, ha! that is a good joke!" roared the peasant. "Wine in my house, indeed! I only wish it were true!"

"Tell your wife to look behind the chest, and I'll warrant you she will find it."

Very unwillingly the dame went to the place indicated, and came back with the bottle of wine. She tried to look as surprised as her husband, but only succeeded in pulling a very wry mouth.

"Bring glasses, wife!" cried the peasant in great good humour. "We must drink the health of this famous oracle. Do you think you can make him speak again, friend?"

"Certainly," said the drummer, beating another tattoo upon the drum. Once again the bees began to hum loudly, and he leant down, pretending to listen to what they had to say.

"Well? Well?" cried the peasant impatiently.

"He says that if your wife will look in the cupboard, she will find a roast fowl and a gammon of bacon, which we can eat instead of this dry bread."

"Upon my word, that is a wonderful oracle!" cried the peasant. "Make haste, wife, and look in the cupboard."

The Swarm Of Bees Within Began To Buzz About In Great Commotion

The dame could not refuse to obey, so she brought the good things and set them on the table, but if looks could have killed anybody the drummer would have been a dead man that day. Little heed he paid to her evil glances, however, but applied himself to the food with a good appetite. Before very long, between the two of them, there was nothing left of the chicken but the bones, and of the gammon but the scrag-end.

Beating Another Tattoo Upon The Drum

"Faith," said the peasant, unbuttoning his waistcoat, "that was a better meal than I expected to get this night. Has your oracle any more agreeable surprises for us, good sir. I pray you, make him speak again."

"With all the will in the world," answered the drummer, "but this will be the last occasion, for he only speaks three times a day." Taking up his sticks, he played the war-march of Napoleon on the drum, and the bees accompanied him as before with their loud humming. The peasant leaned forward eagerly to listen, while his wife stood by trembling with fear.

"Ah," said the drummer at last, looking at them both with a grave face. "This time my oracle tells me of a very serious matter. He says that in the big chest over there a big black demon is hidden!"

"What! What!" cried the peasant, jumping up from his chair as though he had been stung. "A demon, did you say?"

"Precisely," answered the drummer. "But don't be alarmed. I will get rid of him for you. Open the door and the windows and then place yourself here, by my side."

The Beadle, Too, Stumbled And Fell

The peasant made haste to do what he was told, and marching boldly up to the chest, the drummer seized the heavy lid and threw it open. Immediately the beadle, who had heard everything and was not a little afraid of his own skin, jumped up, his figure entirely covered with the folds of his black mantle, and ran for the door. So sudden was his appearance, and so hasty his flight, that he ran with full force into the peasant, who had no time to get out of his way, and knocked that worthy man flying head over heels. The beadle, too, stumbled and fell, but quickly recovering himself, made blindly for the door, fell over the folds of his cloak, and tumbled head foremost into the ditch by the side of the road. There was a sudden splashing sound, a muffled murmur, and then silence.

"Poof!" said the peasant, when he had picked himself up and rubbed his limbs. "That was a narrow escape! I saw the demon quite plainly—he was all black, with fiery eyes, and a forked tail! Thank heaven that your oracle warned us, good sir, or he would have devoured us as we slept!"

The next morning, as the drummer and the peasant sat at breakfast, the latter said:

"Will you sell me that oracle of yours, drummer?"

"That depends," answered his guest. "You know it is worth a great deal of money."

"I will give you a hundred crowns," said the peasant, "and that is all I have in the world."

"Very well," said the drummer. "It is little enough for such a wonderful oracle as this is, but I have taken a fancy to you, and I cannot refuse. Give me the money." So the bargain was concluded. Donatus received the hundred crowns, and in return handed over the drum. Then he bade farewell to his host and was just going out of the door when the latter called after him: "Stay a moment—I have just thought of something. How am I to understand the language which the oracle speaks?"

"Oh, that is easy enough," answered Donatus. "Listen while I tell you what to do. At ten o'clock, precisely, not a minute before or a minute afterwards, go and plant your wife in the ground up to her armpits, then smear her face and shoulders with honey. That done, take the oracle with you into the attic where you found me, and having first bandaged your eyes, remove the top skin of the drum. Wait for a quarter of an hour; then replace the skin, and take the drum with you to the place where you left your wife. In that very moment the meaning of the oracle's language will be revealed to you, and you will know as much as I know myself!"

"Many thanks!" cried the peasant delightedly. "Good day to you, soldier, and good luck!"

"And to you!" answered the drummer, and he went away laughing up his sleeve at the fellow's simplicity.

About a mile farther along the road he saw a man working in the fields, and went up to him.

"If you like, gossip," said he, "I'll do a bit of that digging for you."

"With all my heart," answered the labourer, giving up his spade.

"Very well, but let us change clothes, for I do not wish to soil my uniform. Here is a crown for you. Go to the inn and buy yourself a glass of wine. When you return you will be surprised to see how much I have done."

The exchange was made and the labourer departed. Less than half an hour afterwards the sound of hoofs was heard on the road, and looking up, the drummer saw his late host, mounted on horseback, spurring furiously towards him. The man's face was purple with fury and he was muttering threats as to what he would do to the drummer when he caught him. He had faithfully carried out all his instructions, and had truly enough learnt the meaning of the humming noise within the drum. So had his wife; for when he went to her in the garden, he found her with her face and shoulders black with bees!

He Had Faithfully Carried Out All His Instructions

Abreast of the place where the drummer was working the peasant reined in his horse, and cried out, "Hallo, you there. Have you seen a soldier pass by this way?"

"A man, master?" mumbled the drummer.

"I said a soldier, you stupid oaf! A man in a red coat with a most villainous face. Have you seen him, I say?"

"Why, yes," the drummer answered. "He went past here about a quarter of an hour ago and made his way into the wood yonder. You'll never find him, master!" he added, with a grin.

"And why won't I?"

"Because he's gone by a secret way. I saw the road he took, and I know how he means to go, but even if I were to show you the way, you would never overtake him, for you would lose yourself in the wood."

"I'll give you a crown if you'll help me to find the rascal," cried the peasant.

"A crown! Come now, that's high pay. You must want him very badly!"

"I do indeed, and I'll break every bone in his body when I catch him."

"Here, lend me your horse, master," said the drummer. "I'll catch him for you, and not for a crown neither, but for nothing. I'd like to see him get a good thrashing, for he called me names as he passed by."

"But can you ride?" asked the peasant.

It Was The Labourer Dressed In The Drummer's Clothes

"Can a duck swim?" answered the drummer scornfully. "Dismount quickly or the scoundrel will get away. Wait here for me," he added, as he rode off, "I'll be back in less than half an hour." Off he went at a gallop, smiling to himself. "First of all a hundred crowns, and now a fine steed," thought he. "Come Donatus, your luck is standing you in good stead. It's odds but you'll win through yet!" He reached the wood, entered it, and the peasant waiting by the roadside, heard the sound of his horse's hoofs grow fainter and fainter until at last they died away.

A quarter of an hour passed, half an hour, an hour, but the labourer did not return. The peasant, fuming with impatience, strode up and down the road, slashing at the grass and bushes with his stick. Suddenly he heard footsteps, and saw a man in a red coat approaching. It was the labourer dressed in the drummer's clothes, who had drunk, not one, but several glasses of wine, and was now returning very pleased with himself and all the world. As he came he trilled out a merry song.

"You knave! You villain!" cried the peasant, throwing himself upon him. "Where are my hundred crowns? What! you would teach me the language of the bees, would you?—and my poor wife is stung all over, and cannot see out of her eyes. Rascal! Scoundrel! Oh, you scum! Take that, and that, and that!" And with each word, he lifted his heavy stick and brought it down heavily upon the shoulders of the unfortunate labourer.

"Here, hold hard, master!" cried the man, twisting and turning to get away. "What's the meaning of this? I'll have the law on you if you don't leave me alone! *Ouch*, give over I tell you! What do I know about your hundred crowns or your wife?"

"What!" cried the peasant, laying on harder than before. "Do you add lying to your other crimes? You will tell me next you have never seen a drum!" And with one last mighty cut he stretched the unfortunate fellow at his feet. Then, for the first time, he had a full view of his face, and saw that he was not the man he took him for.

"Was there ever such an unlucky man in all the world as I?" he moaned, as he turned wearily homeward, pursued by the curses and threats of the man he had beaten. "First I lose a hundred crowns, and then the love of my wife, who will never forgive me her injuries; and now, into the bargain, I have lost my horse! God forgive that drummer, and protect him if ever he falls into my hands!"

I wish I could tell you that the unlucky peasant's desire was fulfilled, and that the drummer met with his deserts. Unhappily my story ends here, and I do not know for certain what happened to him, but people do say that he never came out of the wood, but rode straight into a marsh and was drowned. If this is true, I am sure that nobody will be sorry!

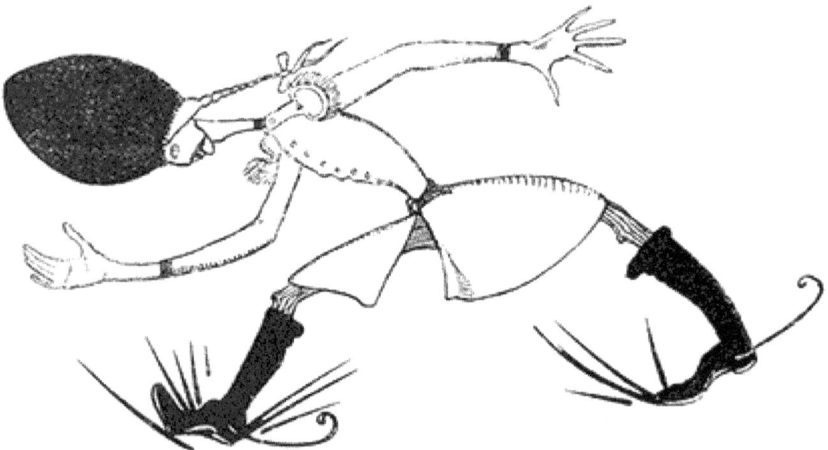

Rode Straight Into A Marsh

When The Fifty Rooks Began To Fly He Could Not Get Free

THE DRUNKEN ROOKS

IT was the middle of winter and the ground was covered with snow. Along the high road came Mynheer Van Ash, the well-known merchant of Alost, driving to the town with two immense casks of the liquor known as Hollands, in which he traded. All unknown to the merchant, one of the casks had a hole in it, and as he drove along the liquor leaked out, and sank into the snow.

In a field close by the roadside were a flock of fifty rooks, who were eagerly turning up the snow and pecking at the ground beneath in search of food. Attracted by the strong and heady smell of the spilt liquor, they flew across to investigate, and having tasted some of the gin-sodden snow, liked it so well that they followed in the train of the cart, eating more and more of it, until at last they were so drunk that they could hardly stand on their feet. Away they went to the fields again, and very soon afterwards the whole flock of them was fast asleep.

Presently, Little Pol, a peasant who worked in the neighbourhood, happened to cross the field on his way homeward, and saw the crows lying stiff and silent on the snow.

"Ah!" said he to himself. "Here is a funny sight! Fifty crows frozen to death with the cold. I'll take them home with me and pluck them. Rook-pie is excellent eating, and such a find is welcome these hard times!" So, taking a cord from his pocket, he set to work to gather up all the rooks, and tie them together by the legs.

This done, he proceeded on his way, dragging the rooks behind him.

The roughness of the motion and the friction of the snow very soon aroused the rooks from their slumber. They all woke up, and finding their legs tied, began to flap their wings together with admirable precision. Unfortunately for Little Pol, he had taken the precaution of fastening the cord to the belt round his middle, so when the fifty rooks began to fly he could not get free, and found himself being lifted into the air.

Up went the fifty rooks cawing and crying, and up too went Little Pol, calling in vain for help. They reached the clouds; they penetrated the clouds; they disappeared from sight.

And since that day not a sign has ever been seen either of the fifty rooks or of Little Pol.

The Rooks

The Battle Of The Birds And Beasts

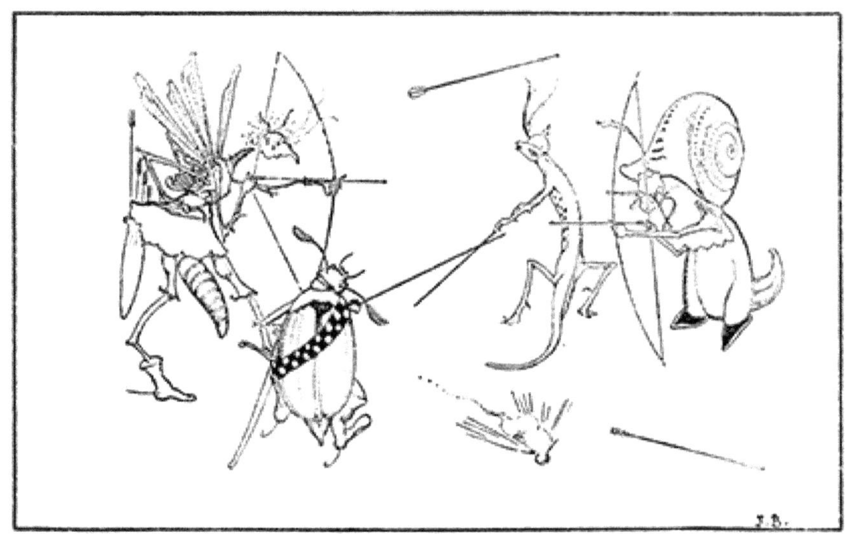

Fighting

THE BATTLE OF THE BIRDS AND BEASTS

ONE day as Bruin the Bear and Isengrim the Wolf were taking a walk in the woods they came to a big elm-tree with a hollow trunk. Peering within in the hope of finding something to eat they espied a little nest supported by two notches in the bark. It was the tiniest and neatest little house one could wish to see, made of fresh green moss, with a small opening in the middle for a door, and was, in fact, the home of a little bird called the Golden-crested Wren. Now among the country people the golden-crested wren is often known by the name of the Kinglet, and being aware of this, Isengrim saw a chance of playing a joke upon his companion. "Look at this nest, Bruin," said he. "What would you say if I told you it was a King's palace?"

"That a King's palace!" laughed Bruin scornfully. "A handful of moss in a hole! Why, with one tap of my paw I could smash it to fragments!"

"I should not advise you to do any such thing," said Isengrim. "The King who lives in that palace is much more powerful than you think, and unless you are looking for trouble it would be best to leave his home alone."

"What!" cried Bruin, in a rage. "Am I to be defied by a miserable little fowl in my own forest? That for your King!" And with one sweep of his paw, he reduced the nest to a shapeless heap of moss. "Now let him revenge himself if he can," he roared. "I hereby declare war upon him and upon all his tribe. Fur against feather! The four-legged animals against those that go on wings. We will put this matter to the test!"

When the Kinglet came home and found his nest destroyed he danced and chattered with anger. Isengrim lost no time in letting him know who was responsible for the mischief, and took a spiteful joy in telling him of the Bear's challenge.

"Very well," said the little wren. "Kinglet is my name, and King shall be my nature. I will call all the winged creatures together and we will settle the matter by the test of arms."

During the next two or three weeks there was a great coming and going in the forest as the two armies assembled. The air was full of the whirl and rustle of wings. From the nests under sunny banks came the wasps in thousands, each with his shining cuirass of black and yellow, and his deadly sting. The gadfly came too, and the tiny gnat, and the mosquito from the stagnant pools, with insects of every other sort and kind—more than one could count in a day. From his eyrie on the mountain crags the lordly eagle came swooping to take his place beside the nightingale and the sparrow. In that hour of need all rivalries were forgotten; the falcon and the hawk took their place in the ranks with the thrush and the robin.

The Kinglet Warned Him To Be Very Careful Not To Buzz

The Bear, on his side, was not idle. Swift-footed messengers were sent to every part of the land to summon the four-legged animals to arms. Slinking through the undergrowth came Isengrim's kin, the grey wolves, with lean flanks and fierce eyes shining. Reynard brought his troop of foxes. Crashing through the trees came the mighty elephants, waving their trunks and trumpeting defiance to the foe. Out of the mud of river-beds, from the grassy plains, and the densest thickets of the forest, the animals came flocking—lions, tigers, camels, bulls, horses—if I were to name them all I should fill this book with their names. Never had so many animals been brought together since the days of Noah's Ark.

When everything was ready, the Kinglet, who was a prudent leader, sent out a spy to try to gain information about the enemy's plans. For this purpose he chose the mosquito, who, as you may imagine, was neither easily seen nor easily caught, particularly as the Kinglet warned him to be very careful not to buzz. Under cover of the darkness he flew to the Bear's camp, and succeeded in discovering the headquarters of the general staff, where the leaders of the animal army were conferring. Just as the mosquito arrived, the Bear and the Fox were speaking together.

"So it is settled," the Bear was saying. "Our great offensive will begin to-morrow. Each of you knows what to do, I think? We have discussed everything, and nothing remains to do, but to press forward to a glorious victory."

"You are right, my lord," said Reynard, "but there is just one thing you have forgotten. How are we to know when the victory is won? We must have a standard-bearer."

"Of course," answered the Bear, "we must have a standard-bearer. I was just going to say so. Who shall it be?"

"With all respect, my lord," answered Reynard, "I propose that it should be I. My beautiful bushy tail will serve as a battle-flag. I will walk at the head of the army and hold my tail straight up in the air, as stiff as a poker. So long as I keep it like that, you will know that all is well; but if anything disastrous should happen, I will let it droop to the ground, so that our troops may have ample warning to take refuge in flight."

"Excellent," said Bruin. "You have heard what Reynard proposes. Take notice that I hereby appoint him standard-bearer to our armies."

So it was agreed, and having learnt all that he wished to know, the mosquito flew back to the Kinglet with his news. The Kinglet said nothing, but sent for the wasp, and gave him certain orders.

At dawn the next morning the great offensive began, and from the very beginning things went rather badly for the armies of the winged animals. At two points of the line the Bear and the Tiger led dashing attacks against divisions commanded by the eagle and the hawk, and after long and fierce fighting, forced them to retire. High upon a knoll commanding the battlefield, in full view of the troops, stood the Fox, with his bushy tail held proudly in the air. As he watched the struggle his lips curled in a grin of triumph.

The Great Offensive Began

Suddenly there was a piercing yell that rang out clear above the noise of battle. It came from the Fox, who drooped his tail to the ground, and ran, howling with pain, to the rear.

"We are lost! We are lost!" cried the animals, seeing the standard lowered.

"Traitors are amongst us! Fly for your lives!" From point to point of the swaying battle-line the panic spread, throwing the army into hopeless confusion. Before long the whole of the Bear's troops were in retreat, and the victorious army of the winged-creatures swept on and over them.

Late that night Bruin the Bear and Isengrim the Wolf, both of them very bedraggled and wearied with much running, sat together gloomily in a distant part of the wood. Presently they saw Reynard the Fox limping towards them, and immediately they rose and began to heap reproaches upon him.

"Traitor!" said Bruin. "Why did you lower the standard? In another hour we should have won."

The Fox looked at them sulkily. "Why did I lower the standard?" said he. "Because a wasp came and stung me right at the root of my tail!"

The Fox

The Cat Rushed Out Of The Room

THE END OF THE WORLD

ONCE upon a time an old woman sat spinning in a room at the top of a high tower. Beneath her chair Chaton, her cat, lay peacefully sleeping. All of a sudden the spinning-wheel jarred and made a loud creaking sound. Startled out of his sleep, Chaton the Cat rushed out of the room and bolted down the stairs as though a thousand demons were at his heels.

In the yard he passed the house-dog who was sitting in front of his kennel. "Hallo, Chaton!" cried the dog. "Where are you going to in such a hurry?"

"I am fleeing the country," answered Chaton. "I have just heard the sounding of the last trump! The end of the world is at hand!"

"If that is so," said the dog, "I would like to run away too. May I come with you?"

"Certainly," answered Chaton. "Seat yourself on my beautiful curly tail." So the dog perched himself on the cat's tail, and off they went together.

A little farther on they came to the farm-gate, and there, perched on the top-most rail, was the cock.

"Whither away, Chaton?" asked the cock. "You seem to be in haste."

"Yes," said Chaton. "I have heard the last trump, which proves that the world is coming to an end, and I want to get safely away before that happens."

"Take me with you, Chaton dear," said the cock.

"By all means," answered the cat. "Jump on to my beautiful curly tail beside the dog." So the cock perched himself on Chaton's tail, and now there were two passengers.

Away went the cat even faster than before, so as to make up for lost time, and presently they passed a rabbit who was nibbling the grass in a field.

"Chaton, Chaton," cried the rabbit, "why are you running so quickly?"

"Don't stop me!" answered the cat. "I've heard the last trump! The end of the world is coming!"

"Oh, dear me!" cried the rabbit. "What an unfortunate thing! Don't leave me here, Chaton, for I am afraid to face the end of the world."

"Very well," said Chaton. "Jump on to my beautiful curly tail with the dog and the cock, and I'll take you with me." So the rabbit also perched himself on the cat's tail, and now there were three of them riding there.

Off went the cat again, but not so quickly this time, because of the weight on his tail, and before very long he came to a pond by the side of which a goose was standing.

"Now then, now then, what's the hurry?" asked the goose. "If you run so fast you'll overheat your blood and die of a fever."

"It's all very well to scoff," answered the cat, "but you must know that the end of the world is coming. I have heard the last trump sound!"

"My goodness!" said the goose. "This is dreadful! Take me with you, Chaton, and I'll be grateful for ever."

"Very well," said the cat. "Jump on to my beautiful curly tail with the dog and the fox and the rabbit." So the goose also perched herself on the cat's tail, so now there were four passengers, and that made five altogether who were running away to escape the end of the world.

All that day the cat kept on running, and towards dusk they came to a forest.

"This seems a good place to rest," said Chaton. "Now then, master cock, fly to the top of a tree and see if you can espy a house in which we can take shelter."

The cock flew to the top of a high tree and from there he saw a number of lights twinkling in the distance. The five fugitives thereupon set off in the direction from which the lights shone, and before long they came to a little village. All the people of the village had left their houses and were gathered together in the square, round a man dressed all in red, with a big red feather in his cap, who was addressing them.

Chaton and his companions pressed close to the edge of the crowd and were just in time to hear these words: "Whoever finds the ring," said the man with the red feather, "and places it on the table in my palace to-morrow before dawn, shall have the five bags of gold which hang on my saddle bow." Having said this, the man in red mounted his horse and rode away.

The Cat, The Dog, The Cock, The Rabbit, And The Goose

Chaton went up to a little peasant who was standing in the crowd. "Tell me, gossip," said he, "who is the man with the red feather, and what's all this about a ring and five bags of gold?"

"Why," said the peasant, "the man in red is the King of this country. He had a valuable ring which was kept in a tiny wooden case on the table by his bed. This afternoon a magpie flew in through the window, snatched up the case, and bore it away to its nest in the topmost boughs of the walnut tree on the village green. The King wants his ring back again, and will give the five bags of gold to anybody who will recover it for him."

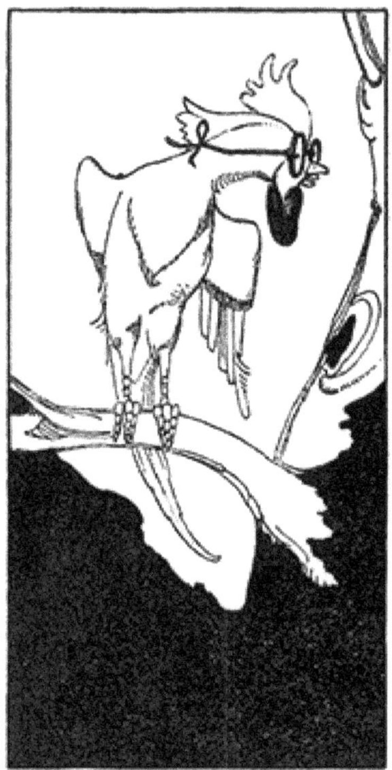

"See If You Can Espy A House"

"I see," said Chaton; "and why don't *you* climb the walnut-tree and get the ring?"

"Because I have too much respect for my neck," answered the peasant, "and so has everybody else here. The boughs at the top of the tree where the nest is are so thin and slender that they would not bear the weight of a child, let alone a grown man. Gold is good, but whole limbs are better, that's what I say!"

"And I!" "And I!" echoed other villagers who had been listening to this conversation.

"In my belief you are quite right," said Chaton seriously. "Let the King risk his own life if he is so anxious to recover his ring." But afterwards, when he had withdrawn with his companions to the shelter of the wood, he sang a different tune.

"My friends," said he, "our fortunes are made! As soon as all is quiet I will climb the tree and get the ring; then you shall sit on my tail again and we'll all go off together to the King's palace and get the bags of gold!" He danced for joy, and the dog and the cock and the goose and the rabbit danced with him.

"Jump On To My Beautiful Curly Tail"

An hour afterwards the cat climbed the tree and came down safely with the little wooden box. The rabbit gnawed it open with his teeth, and sure enough there was the ring inside it.

"Now," said Chaton, "we will all go to the King's palace, but I am very tired with running all day. I propose that the dog takes a turn at carrying us." This was agreed. The other four got on to the dog's back and clung there while he ambled off as fast as he could along the road towards the palace.

The Other Four Got On To The Dog's Back

Just before dawn they came to a wide river. Now it was the turn of the goose to work for the common good. She was quite used to the water, and one by one she took the other animals across on her back. Shortly afterwards they arrived at the King's palace, and the cock flew up through the open window of the King's room with the ring in his beak, and placed it on the table by the bed. Then he awoke the King with a loud crow and claimed the reward, which was willingly given.

In great glee at their good fortune the animals went on their way, each with his bag of gold, and every one of them had by this time quite forgotten his fear about the coming of the end of the world. They went on and on until they came to a place where five ways met. Then Chaton said: "Here we are at the parting of the ways. Let us each choose a road, and part good friends."

At this moment there came along a pig with a knife and fork stuck in his back. In his right ear was salt; in his left ear pepper, and mustard was on his tail, so that everybody who was hungry had only to cut themselves a slice of meat and sit down to feast.

Our friends gladly availed themselves of this good chance, and I who tell you this story would willingly have done the same, but as soon as I went up to the pig, he ran at me with his head down and sent me flying through the air, and through the window of my house, where I fell into the chair in which I am now sitting, finishing this story of the wonderful adventures of Chaton, the Dog, the Cock, the Rabbit, and the Goose.

Sent Me Flying Through The Air

The Dragon

THE REWARD OF THE WORLD

IN days of old, when there were dragons in the land, a youthful knight was riding along the high road. It was a beautiful summer day, and the sun shone so warmly that the rider presently began to feel thirsty, so coming to a clear stream of water, he swung himself from the saddle and went to drink. As he parted the bushes to get to the water he heard a strange rumbling and roaring sound, and looking quickly in the direction from which it came he saw to his horror an immense dragon lying by the water-side pinned down by a huge mass of rock which had rolled down upon the creature as it came to drink.

The knight's first impulse was to flee, for it is better not to meddle with dragons, even when accident has rendered them helpless, but before he could regain his horse the creature saw him, and cried, "Good knight, come and help me, I pray you, to escape from my miserable position. This rock upon my back is slowly crushing me to death."

The knight hesitated, and was in two minds what to do between his fear of the dragon and his pity for its unfortunate plight. Seeing this, the creature called out again, saying, "If you will only set me free I will repay you richly, for I will give you *The Reward of the World*."

"The Reward of the World," thought the knight, "that will indeed be worth having!" for he had often heard that dragons were the guardians of immense treasures. So, overcoming his fright, he went up to the creature, and at the cost of great exertion managed to roll away the stone that was pressing on its back.

"Poof! That's better," said the dragon, blowing a cloud of smoke out of its nostrils. "I had begun to think I was doomed to stay in that place for ever!" He rubbed his sore back reflectively with one scaly paw, and looked at the knight, who stood waiting.

"Well?" said he.

"You promised me *The Reward of the World*!" said the knight.

"Did I so?" asked the dragon, still tenderly stroking his back. "Well, you shall have it!" And suddenly he launched himself upon the knight, winding his horrible coils around his body, and almost crushing him to death. The unfortunate young man struggled feebly, but he was powerless in the grip of the monster.

"Your promise!" he gasped. "Is this my reward for having saved your life?"

"Certainly," replied the dragon. "This is *The Reward of the World*. I am keeping my word!"

"I don't believe you," said the knight. "It is a trick to excuse your treachery. What a fool I was to trust a dragon's word!"

"It is just as I say," the dragon replied. "But I confess I owe you something, and I should hate to eat you feeling that you had a grievance. I'll tell you what I'll do. I'll submit this question to the first three people we meet along the road, and if they decide in my favour you must accept the verdict. Is it agreed?"

"Agreed," said the knight, who was glad of any chance to escape from the dragon's coils, so the creature released him, and the two set off together down the road.

They had not gone far before they met the dog.

"Stay a moment, master dog," said the knight. "What do you understand by *The Reward of the World*?"

The dog replied, "When I was young I was a splendid watch-dog, and guarded my master's house against all comers. In those days everybody made a fuss of me. I had plenty of good food to eat, and my own particular place before the fire. Now, alas! I am old. My sight is so weak and my powers so feeble that I can no longer work for my living, and in consequence everybody kicks me out of their way. I eat what I can get, which is not much. Even the children throw stones at me, knowing that my teeth are not sharp enough to bite, and wherever I go people say, 'There is that beastly hound again! Chase him away with a stick!' That is *The Reward of the World*."

There was little comfort for the knight in this, nevertheless he did not give up hope, but accosted the next creature they met, which happened to be a horse.

"What is *The Reward of the World*?" the knight asked him.

"Listen," said the horse bitterly, "and I will tell you. All my life I have laboured diligently for one master. Day in and day out I dragged his cart to market, working myself to skin and bone in his service. Now I am grown old and my strength begins to fail, so that I can no longer earn my keep. To-day I heard him say that he was going to send me to the knackers' yard and sell my poor old carcass for a couple of crowns. That is *The Reward of the World*, young master, and may heaven preserve you from it!"

An Immense Dragon Lying By The Water-Side

"You see!" said the dragon, as the two went on, "my words are already justified. Come, be sensible and let me eat you without further ado!"

"My Sight Is So Weak And My Powers So Feeble"

"No," said the knight, "we have still one person to ask. Here comes a fox. Let us see what he has to say about the matter. Reynard, what do you understand by *The Reward of the World*?"

"How do you mean?" asked the fox. "What is the case in point?"

"Well, you see," explained the knight, "I found this dragon in a position of uncommon peril, and he promised, if I would rescue him, to give me *The Reward of the World*. The question now arises as to what *The Reward of the World* is."

"I see," said Reynard thoughtfully. "His life was in danger, you say? How was that?"

"A huge stone had fallen on to his back, pinning him down so that he could not move. I rolled the stone away, and set him free."

The fox scratched his head and pondered. "If you don't mind," said he, "I'd rather like to have this matter made a little clearer. Where did all this happen?"

"A little farther back along the road, by the side of the stream."

"I'll come and look at the place!"

So the knight led Reynard to the banks of the stream, where he stood gazing for a time at the big stone.

"I want to be quite sure I understand all the circumstances," said he at last. "Does the dragon mind getting under the stone again for a moment, so that I can see exactly how he lay?"

"Does The Dragon Mind Getting Under The Stone Again?"

"Not at all," said the dragon politely, and he lay down on the bank, while the knight and the fox together rolled the stone on top of him.

"Splendid!" said Reynard, when the dragon was safely pinned down. "Now everything is as it was before!" Then turning to the knight, he added, "If you, knowing what you know now, care to release him again, you are at liberty to do so, but...." And he winked slyly. There was no need to say more.

"I am really very much obliged to you," said the knight, as he walked off down the road with Reynard, leaving the dragon still under the stone. "That was a capital idea of yours, and it certainly saved my life. I would like to show my gratitude in some way, and I shall be honoured if you will accept my hospitality for a few days."

Reynard needed no pressing, but went home with the young man there and then, and thoroughly enjoyed the good fare with which he was provided. Since, however, a fox is always a fox, no matter what company he is in, Master Reynard could not forbear from stealing, and every night he crept into the hen-house and killed one or two chickens. When the knight discovered this he was very angry, and picking up a big stick he gave the fox a good thrashing and drove him forth.

"That is *The Reward of the World*," he said to himself, as he watched Reynard disappearing into the distance. But whether he was referring to the way the fox had treated him, or to his own treatment of the fox, I cannot say.

Two Foxes

Nothing Was Left Of The Fishes

ONE BAD TURN BEGETS ANOTHER

TYBERT the Cat and Courtoys the Dog were very great friends—that is to say they were as friendly as their natures would let them be. Both of them were exceedingly greedy and selfish. The Cat was spiteful and the Dog was sullen. Master Tyb was always willing to give up to the dog what he did not need himself, and on his part, Courtoys never stole the cat's food while the cat was looking. Neither was loath to play a mean trick upon the other if he could do so without injury to himself, but except for these little matters they were quite in accord, and very friendly, as I said before, and on the whole they got on very well together.

There came a time when, in spite of Tybert's shyness and Courtoys' strength, they could by no means find anything to eat. For two days not a morsel of food had passed the lips of either; and this made them very bad tempered.

"I wish I'd never seen you," said Courtoys to Tyb. "A fine partner you are, upon my word, when you can't find food for us. Where are those wonderful wits of yours, of which you are always boasting."

"In my head," answered Tyb spitefully. "And such as they are, they have to do duty for two. If you'd talk less, and think more, and use your eyes, we would be better off. Here is a cart coming along the road; perhaps we shall find our dinner inside it!"

Sure enough, a heavy wagon was rumbling along the road towards them, driven by a peasant with a round and rather stupid face. As it came nearer, Tyb and Courtoys sniffed the air, and the water ran out of the corners of their mouths.

"Fish," said Tybert ravenously.

"Fish!" echoed Courtoys. "Here's a chance to exercise those wits of yours. How can we get it?"

"I have a plan," answered the Cat. "Come quickly and hide yourself with me in the ditch until the wagon has passed, and I will tell you all about it!"

So it was done. The wagon rumbled by, the scent of the fish with which it was laden filling the air, and the driver went on calmly smoking his pipe, little dreaming that four hungry eyes were gazing at him through the bushes that bordered the side of the road.

"Now then," cried Tybert, "our time has come. Follow the wagon and don't let it out of your sight for a moment, but take care that the driver does not see you. I shall go on in front and stretch myself out on the road, pretending to be dead. It's odds but what the driver, seeing me lying there, will covet my skin, and will pick me up and throw me into the cart. Once there, I'll throw the fish out to you, and you will know what to do with it."

"Oh, yes, I'll know what to do with it," said Courtoys to himself, with a grin, and, keeping well out of sight of the driver, he followed the wagon.

Tybert's plan worked to perfection. He ran on for about a quarter of a mile, keeping to the fields bordering the road, and then stretched himself out at full length, with his mouth open as though he were dead.

"Oho!" said the peasant, as he drove up. "What's this? A dead cat! I'll take him with me, and sell his skin for a few sous. This time next week some fine lady will be wearing him round her neck, thinking he's sable." And with that he dismounted, picked up the cat and slung him carelessly into the wagon on top of the heap of fish.

Hardly was he back in his place, than Tybert arose and began to pick out the biggest and fattest fish and throw them into the road. He had to be very careful in doing this, because now and again the peasant turned his head. Once when a very big fish was tumbled out, the noise of its fall aroused the peasant, who swung round sharply, and Tybert was only just in time to avert discovery by laying himself out and pretending to be dead as before.

When he had thrown out what he considered was a sufficient quantity, Tybert rested awhile, so that the dog could collect the spoils, and then jumped from the wagon to go and claim his share. When he came up to Courtoys, however, he found to his dismay that nothing was left of the fish but a heap of bones.

"That was a splendid plan of yours, brother," said Courtoys, licking his lips. "The fish were delicious, and I hardly feel hungry at all now! Do make haste and take your share!" And he waved his paw invitingly towards the heap of bones. Tybert gave him one look, and then grinned as though in enjoyment of an excellent joke. Not by word or action did he give any sign of the anger which was consuming him, but he determined to have his revenge.

The Biggest And Fattest Fish

A day or two later his chance came. Lurking in his usual stealthy way in a farmyard, he saw the farmer go into the house with a fine big ham, which he hung by a cord on a nail in the kitchen wall. Away he ran to Courtoys and told him what he had seen.

"Well," said Courtoys surlily, "and what about it?"

"Why," answered Tybert. "There is no reason why we should not feast on that ham, you and I. It will be the easiest thing in the world to steal it. The latch of the kitchen window is broken, and it cannot be locked. All you have to do is to go there to-night, creep through the window, pull down the ham, and throw it out to me."

Stretched Himself Out At Full Length

"Why can't you get it yourself?" asked Courtoys suspiciously.

"Ah," said the cat, "I am not strong enough to pull it down."

"And what about the farmer's dogs? I seem to remember hearing they are savage brutes!"

"Well, of course, if you're *afraid* ..." answered the cat disdainfully.

"Afraid yourself!" cried Courtoys. "You leave this to me."

So that very night, when the moon had set, the two crept into the farmyard, and the dog managed to get through the window into the kitchen unobserved. The next moment he had pulled down the ham and had thrown it out of the window to Tybert, who was waiting below. Tybert seized it in his mouth and ran off, but as soon as he reached the gate he gave a series of such blood-curdling miaows, that he roused every dog on the farm. Out they came, hair bristling, and teeth flashing, just in time to catch our friend Courtoys as he jumped down from the window.

Then occurred a ferocious fight. With his back to the wall Courtoys put up a sturdy resistance, but he was very badly mangled indeed before he managed to escape. With one ear torn off and one eye closed, bleeding from many wounds and panting with his exertions, he limped painfully up to where the cat awaited him.

"My poor friend," cried Tybert. "Are you badly hurt? Never mind, the ham was worth it—it simply melted in the mouth. I have already eaten my share, and I willingly give you yours!" So saying, he pointed to the greasy string by which the ham had been suspended, and which was now all that remained. Courtoys gazed at it blankly.

"You see," explained Tybert calmly, as he prepared to take his departure, "a cord is worth a good many fishbones!"

"I Willingly Give You Yours!"

"Why Are You Blowing Your Soup?"

THE PEASANT AND THE SATYRS

ONE cold winter's day a peasant set out on a journey which led him through the depths of a forest into which he had not hitherto been. The result was that he lost his way, and after wandering about for many hours in the hope of finding it again, he found himself, just as dusk was coming on, in a little clearing where he was overjoyed to see a small house with a cheerful light in the window. "Here is a chance of supper and a bed," thought the peasant, and he made haste to go up to the cottage door.

Now this house in the clearing was not inhabited by men, but by some strange forest folk who were called satyrs. If you want to know what they were like, you must look at the pictures. Certainly the peasant had never seen anything like them before, although he had often heard of them, and when he nearly tumbled over the little satyr children who were playing in the snow outside the house door, he was the most surprised man in all those parts. It was too late to draw back however, so he went boldly up to the door and gave a loud knock.

"Come in!" cried a gruff voice, and the peasant accordingly went in and found himself facing the Father of all the Satyrs, who had a long beard and a pair of horns jutting from his forehead. The poor fellow's knees trembled underneath him for fright, especially when he saw all the other satyrs, the mother and the uncles and the aunts, glowering at him.

"Please forgive me for my intrusion," said he, "but I have lost my way in the woods, and I am half dead with hunger and cold. It would be an act of great kindness if you would give me some food and allow me to take shelter for the night."

So saying, to give point to his remarks, he set to work to blow upon his chilled fingers, which indeed were blue with the cold.

"Why are you blowing your fingers?" asked the Father of all the Satyrs curiously.

"Why, to warm them," answered the peasant, and he blew harder than before.

"Well, sit down," said the Satyr. "As it happens we are just about to have supper, and you are welcome to share it with us."

So the peasant sat down to supper, and all the Satyr family sat down too, and watched him with big unblinking eyes, so that he felt very uncomfortable. A big basin of soup was set before him, and finding it very hot, he began to blow upon it.

At this all the Satyr family cried out in surprise, and the Father Satyr said, "Why are you blowing your soup?"

"To cool it," answered the peasant. "It is too hot, and I am afraid it may scald my mouth."

Another and a louder cry of surprise came from all the Satyrs, but the Father cried out loudest of all, and seemed very indignant. "Come," he said, advancing to the peasant and taking him by the collar. "Out you go! There is no place in my house for a man who can blow hot and cold with the same breath. That smells too much of sorcery or magic. Out you go, I say, and practise your spells in the forest."

So the poor peasant had to go supperless and spend the night in the woods, with no shelter but the trees, and the snow for coverlet.

And, if you wish to know when all this happened, all I can tell you is that it was a very long time ago, in the days when fishes flew, and cats had wings.

The Satyrs' Village

"There Is No Place In My House For A Man Who Can Blow Hot And Cold"

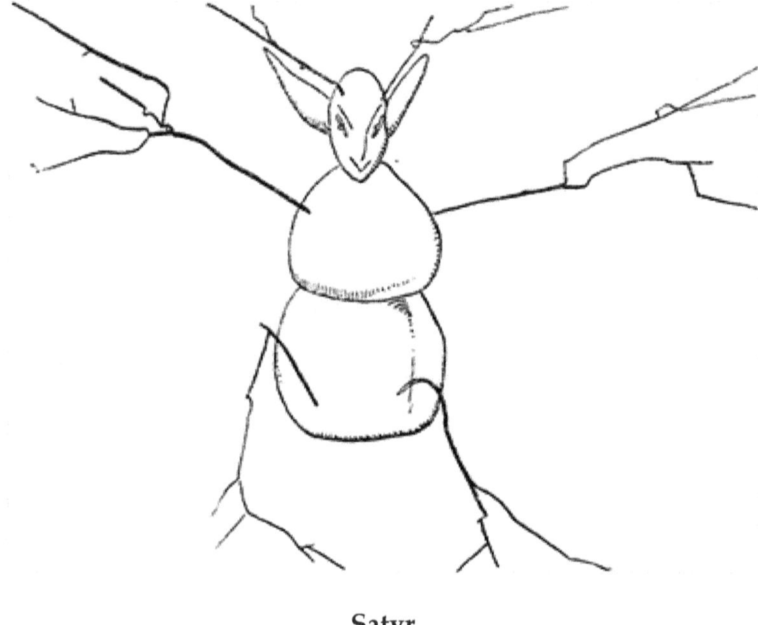

Satyr

The Two Friends

THE TWO FRIENDS AND THE BARREL OF GREASE

A DOG and a wolf who were very great friends set up house together, and agreed to share equally any food they might obtain. One day they managed to steal a barrel of grease from the house of a countryman who lived close by, and having no immediate need of it, they decided to put it away until the winter, when they might be glad of anything they could get to appease their hunger. So the barrel of grease was carefully hidden away in the cellar.

All went well for some time, and then the wolf began to think longingly of the hidden store. Every time he thought of the grease he imagined himself licking it up, and at last he could withstand the temptation no longer, so he went to the dog and said: "I shall be out all day to-morrow. A cousin of mine has just had a little son, and he has sent for me to go and be godfather at the christening."

"Very well, my friend," answered the dog. "Go by all means. They have paid you a great honour by asking you, and of course you cannot refuse."

The wolf departed, but he went no farther than the cellar, where he spent the whole of the day by the barrel of grease, eating and eating until he could hold no more. Late at night he returned, licking his chops, and the dog said: "Well, my friend, did everything go off well?"

"Splendidly, thank you!" answered the wolf.

"Good! And what name did they give the child?"

"Oh," said the wolf, thinking of the barrel of grease, "they called him *Begun*."

"What a strange name!" cried the dog, "I never heard the like of it in my life. However, every one to his taste!"

A day or two later the wolf once again began to think of the delicious food in the cellar, so he told the dog that he had just received another summons from a different cousin, who also had a baby to which she wished him to stand godfather. "I wish to goodness they would leave me alone!" he said, pretending to be very much annoyed. "Anybody would think that I had nothing else to do but to stand godfather to other people's brats!"

"You shouldn't be so good-natured," laughed the dog. "It is clear that you make a very good godfather, or you would not be so much in demand."

Away went the wolf and spent a second satisfying day with the barrel of grease. When he returned the dog asked him the name of the child.

"*Half-Done*," said the wolf.

"Bah!" cried the dog, "that is an even sillier name than the other. I can't think what parents are coming to—in my time plain Jean or Jacques was good enough for anybody."

The wolf made no reply, being in fact fast asleep, for he had dined very well, and was drowsy. A day or two afterwards however, he played the same trick again, and devoured the last of the fat in the barrel. This time, when asked the name of the child to whom he had stood godfather, he answered: "*All-done*."

The dog had no suspicion of the way he had been deceived, and all went well until the winter came and food became difficult to procure. Then one day the dog said: "It seems to me that the time has come to tap our barrel of grease. What do you say, friend? Weren't we wise to put it away for a time like this!"

"I believe you," answered the wolf.

"Come then, let us go to the cellar and enjoy the fruits of our prudence."

So off they went to the cellar, where they found the barrel in the very place they had left it, but with nothing inside it. The dog looked at the wolf, and the wolf looked at the dog, and of the two the wolf seemed the more surprised.

"What's this?" cried the dog. "Where has our grease gone?" Then, looking at the wolf suspiciously: "This is some of your work, my friend!"

"Oh, indeed!" said the wolf, "and since when has it been proved that dogs do not like grease?"

"You mean to accuse me of stealing it?" cried the dog angrily.

"One of the two of us must have taken it, for nobody else knew it was here!"

"It was certainly not I."

"Well," said the wolf, "it is no use squabbling over the matter. Fortunately there is a way of discovering which of us is the culprit. Obviously the one who has eaten all that grease must be absolutely full of fat. Let us both go to sleep in the sunshine. At the end of an hour or two the heat will melt the grease which will soak through and show on the body of the one who is the thief."

"Where Has All Our Grease Gone?"

Feeling quite secure in his innocence, the dog willingly agreed to this plan, and the two went out and lay down in a sheltered place, where the heat of the sun was strong. After a time the dog began to yawn, and in less than half an hour he was sound asleep, but the wolf had a good reason for not following his example, and although he closed his eyes to deceive his friend, he remained wide awake.

Presently, having made sure that the dog was slumbering peacefully, he arose and tiptoed softly down to the cellar. There he collected with his long tongue, every bit of the grease that still remained sticking to the sides and bottom of the barrel, and returning to the sleeper, carefully smeared the grease over his jaws, back, and thighs. Several times he did this, until the dog was covered with a thin greasy film. Then he lay down again and once more pretended to sleep.

A little while afterwards the dog woke up, and found the grease all over his body. He could not make out how it got there, and while he was still regarding himself with a look of blank surprise, the wolf cried: "Ah, now we know who was the thief! The grease has betrayed you, my friend!"

The poor dog looked very sheepish, and had not a word to say for himself. He puzzled over the matter until his head ached, and at last he came to the conclusion that he must have been sleep-walking and have stolen the grease without knowing it—a conclusion with which the wolf entirely agreed.

Begun, Half-Done, All-Done

Mrs. Bruin And Reynard

WHY THE BEAR HAS A STUMPY TAIL

ONE very cold winter, when the ground was covered with snow and the ponds and rivers were frozen hard, Reynard the Fox and all the other animals went out to enjoy themselves by sliding and skating on the ice. After a time Reynard began to feel hungry, so he wandered off by himself in search of something to eat. He nosed about here, and he nosed about there; he lay in wait behind bushes in the hope of being able to catch a bird; he lurked by the walls of farmhouses ready to spring out upon any unsuspecting chicken that might show itself, but all in vain. The birds were wary, and the fowls were all safe in the hen-houses.

Disappointed with his lack of success Reynard betook himself to the river, now covered with a glistening sheet of ice, and there, under the shelter of a bank, he found a hole in the ice which had not been frozen over. He sat down to watch the hole, and presently a little fish popped up its head for a breath of air. Reynard's paw darted, and the next moment the unfortunate creature lay gasping on the ice. Fish after fish the fox caught in this way, and when he had quite satisfied his hunger he strung the remainder on a stick and took his departure, not forgetting first of all to offer up a prayer for the repose of his victims.

He had not gone far before he met Mrs. Bruin, who had also come out in search of something to eat. When she saw Reynard with his fine catch of fish, she opened her eyes, I can tell you, and said: "Wherever did you get all those fine fishes from, cousin? They make my mouth water! I am so hungry that I could bite the head off an iron nail!"

"After A Time The Fish Will Come To Bite At It"

"Ah," said Reynard slyly, "wouldn't you just like to know!"

"It is what I'm asking you," said Mrs. Bruin. "You would surely not be so mean as to keep the good news to yourself!"

"I don't know so much about that," answered Reynard, "but I have a certain fondness for you, cousin, so come along with me and I will show you the place where I caught the fish."

Nothing loath, the bear followed, and presently they came to the hole in the ice.

"Do you see that hole, cousin?" said Reynard. "That is where the fish come up to breathe. All you have to do is to sit on the ice and let your tail hang down into the water. After a time the fish will come to bite at it, but don't you move. Sit quite still until the evening; then you will find a score of fishes on your tail and you can pull them out all together."

Mrs. Bruin was delighted with the plan and immediately sat down and dipped her tail into the water.

"That's the way," said Reynard. "Now I'll just be walking home to see to my dinner, but I'll be back presently. Be careful to keep quite still, or you'll spoil everything!"

So for the next three hours Mrs. Bruin sat on the ice with her tail in the water, and very cold it was, but she consoled herself with the thought of the delicious meal she would have when the fish were landed.

Late in the afternoon Reynard returned. "Well, cousin," said he, "how do you feel?"

"Very cold," said Mrs. Bruin, with her teeth chattering. "My tail is so numb that I hardly know I've got one!"

"Does it feel heavy?" asked Reynard anxiously.

"Very heavy," said Mrs. Bruin.

"There must be *hundreds* of fish on it!" said Reynard. He left the bank and walked round the bear, observing that the water in the hole had frozen over, and that Mrs. Bruin's tail was held firmly in the ice.

"I think you may safely pull up now," he went on, "but you must be careful to land all the fish together. There is only one way to do that: you must give a strong, sharp, sudden pull and take them by surprise. Now then, are you ready? One, two, three...!"

At the word three Mrs. Bruin rose on her hind legs and gave a mighty jerk, but her tail was so firmly embedded in the ice that it would not come out.

"My word," cried Reynard, "you have caught the whole river-full. Persevere, cousin—now then, a long pull and a strong pull!"

"Ouf!" grunted Mrs. Bruin, "ouf, ouf ... ah!" And then she suddenly tumbled head over heels on the ice, as with one mighty jerk, she snapped her beautiful bushy tail clean off close to the roots.

"All You Have To Do Is To Sit On The Ice"

When she had gathered her scattered wits together well enough to understand what had happened, she went to look for Reynard, but he had suddenly remembered an important engagement elsewhere, and was not to be found. And from that time down to this every bear has been born with a little stumpy tail.

"One, Two, Three...!"

Born With A Little Stumpy Tail

Margot And The Cat

THE WITCH'S CAT

ONCE upon a time there was a wicked old witch who lived all alone in the topmost chamber of a tall and gloomy tower. There she sat day after day with her ugly head resting on her hands, peering out through a slit in the wall upon the countryside. Her only companion was a big black tom-cat, who sat by her side in the darkened chamber, his eyes shining like green fire in the gloom.

One day as the witch sat there, she saw a little girl gathering berries in the wood. The sight made her show her toothless gums in a malicious grin and she muttered to herself: "Wait there, wait there, my ducky, my darling, till I come to you, for your flesh will be very sweet." Then she put on a long cloak and took a walking-staff in her hand and went down the stairs.

Now the little girl, whose name was Margot, had strayed very far from home in her eagerness to gather the ripe berries, and she was in a part of the country which was quite strange to her. Had she happened to meet anybody on her way they would have warned her not to go near the witch's tower, but she had not met a soul all day, and so she had no idea of the dreadful danger that was threatening her. She went on gathering her berries, light-heartedly humming a tune, until her basket was nearly full, and then she sat down at the foot of a tree to rest.

Presently she saw an old woman coming towards her. It was the witch, who had muffled herself up in her cloak, so that her face could not easily be seen.

"Good-day, my dear," said the witch. "Will you give me a few of those ripe berries?"

"Of course I will," answered Margot. "Take as many as you like, I can easily gather some more." So the witch took a handful of berries, and sat down by Margot's side to eat them. And all the time she was eating she was gazing greedily at the little girl's white neck and rosy cheeks, but Margot could not see the hateful look in the witch's eyes because the cloak hid her face.

"Where do you live, little girl?" asked the witch after a while.

Margot told her, and the witch said: "You must be very tired with walking all that way. If you will come to my house I will give you a bowl of milk and a slice of currant cake, and you shall see all the wonderful things that I keep in my cupboards."

So Margot went with the witch into the gloomy tower, not so much because she wanted the milk or the cake, but to see the pretty things in the cupboards, and no sooner was she within than the witch fell upon her, and bound her fast with a cord, and carried her up to the topmost room, where the cat was sitting blinking its green eyes. Then the old witch opened the door of a dark cupboard, and pushed poor Margot inside, for she meant to keep her there until she had grown bigger and fatter, so that she would make a more satisfying meal. To this end the witch brought her plenty of rich food every day, and from time to time she would feel Margot's arm to see whether she was plump enough to go into the pot. Poor child, how frightened she was, and how miserable at being kept in that dark cupboard all alone. She cried nearly all day long, but there was nobody to hear her except the witch's big black cat, and he was a silent animal who did not show his feelings. Margot was almost as sorry for him as she was for herself, for the witch often beat him unmercifully, and the girl tried to comfort him by giving him pieces from her dinner, which she pushed out through the crack under the door.

One day when the old witch had gone out as usual, leaving Margot a prisoner, the girl was surprised to hear a voice speaking to her from the room beyond. "Margot, Margot," said the voice, "don't cry any more, but listen to me."

"Who are you?" asked the little girl.

"I am the witch's cat," the voice went on. "I am going to push the key of the cupboard underneath the door. Take it and let yourself out, but make haste, for you have no time to waste!"

"Thank you, thank you," said Margot, when she found herself free. "But how is it that you are able to talk? I did not know that cats could speak."

"They can't, as a rule," said the witch's cat, "but never mind that now. The witch may return at any moment, and we must get you safely out of her reach."

"Yes, yes," said Margot, "I must go at once. I will run like the wind!"

"That is no use," said the cat. "Before you had got half-way home the witch would overtake you."

"Then what must I do? Is there anywhere I can hide?"

"When she returns and finds you gone she will ransack every corner of the tower. Not even a mouse could escape her keen eyes."

She Meant To Keep Her There Until She Had Grown Bigger And Fatter

"Oh dear! oh dear!" said Margot, beginning to cry again. "Do help me to escape, kind cat, and I will be grateful to you all my life."

"Of course I will help you," answered the cat, "that is why I let you out of the cupboard. Take this piece of carpet, and when the witch has almost overtaken you, throw it on to the ground and it will turn into a wide river. That will delay her for some time, because she cannot swim, but if she manages to get across, and overtakes you again, throw down this comb, which will immediately change into a dense forest. You may plunge into it without fear, for a way will open before you between the trees, but the witch will have to cut a way through, foot by foot, with her knife; and long before she has done that you will be safely home."

Margot thanked the cat, and having taken the carpet and the comb, she fled swiftly down the stairs.

A short time afterwards the witch came home, and when she discovered that her prisoner had escaped she howled with rage. Mounting to the very roof of the tower, she gazed out upon the countryside, and soon descried the figure of the little girl, running as fast as she could in the direction of her home.

"I'll have you yet," muttered the witch, and away she went after her.

Margot saw her coming, and redoubled her speed, but all to no avail, for the witch gained upon her rapidly. Soon she heard her hissing breath, and looking fearfully over her shoulder, saw the baleful look of triumph in her eyes.

Paddling With Her Broom

Quickly then, Margot took out the strip of carpet and laid it upon the ground. Immediately it turned into a wide and swiftly flowing river. The witch gave a cry of rage, and tried to wade after her, but the flood mounted swiftly, first to her knees, and then to her waist. Another moment and she would have been swept away, but taking a nutshell from her pocket she set it afloat upon the waters, muttering a charm as she did so. Then the nutshell turned into a little boat, into which the old crone pulled herself, and, paddling with her broom, made shift to cross the river.

The delay had given Margot a good start, but the witch wore enchanted boots which enabled her to cover the ground at a wonderful rate. Ten minutes more and she was once again at Margot's heels.

Then the little girl drew out the comb and flung it behind her. Immediately a dense forest sprang up, and Margot fled into it, through an alley that opened itself before her. Spluttering with anger, the witch drew her knife to hack her way through the wood, but long before she had cut a dozen yards Margot was safely home and in her mother's arms.

The old witch made her way back to the tower, and the things she said were so terrible that the very air was poisoned, and the grass by the roadside withered and turned black. No sooner had she set foot within her doorway, however, than she crumbled to dust, and a wind arose and blew the dust to all quarters of the heavens.

So that was the end of the old witch, for her power ceased as soon as one of her victims managed to escape. As for the black cat, nobody ever saw him again, but it was whispered that he was really a Prince whom the wicked old crone had captured years before, and given the shape of a cat by enchantment. By helping Margot to escape he had released himself from the spell that bound him, and was enabled to return to his father's kingdom.

He Was Really A Prince

Lector House believes that a society develops through a two-fold approach of continuous learning and adaptation, which is derived from the study of classic literary works spread across the historic timeline of literature records. Therefore, we aim at reviving, repairing and redeveloping all those inaccessible or damaged but historically as well as culturally important literature across subjects so that the future generations may have an opportunity to study and learn from past works to embark upon a journey of creating a better future.

This book is a result of an effort made by Lector House towards making a contribution to the preservation and repair of original ancient works which might hold historical significance to the approach of continuous learning across subjects.

HAPPY READING & LEARNING!

LECTOR HOUSE LLP
E-MAIL: lectorpublishing@gmail.com

9 789390 294923